Town and Country Creole Cooking

Traditional and Modern Recipes of Haiti

Betty Turnbull
Wally Turnbull

Forward by Elizabeth Turnbull

www.lightmessages.com

International Standard Book Number: 978-0-9679937-9-9

Printed in the United States of America

Town and Country Creole Cooking: Traditional and Modern Recipes of Haiti has been compiled for the entrenched local, adventuresome cook, avid recipe collector, and newcomer to all things Haiti. Our diverse collection of recipes will introduce you to the best of Haiti's cuisine from rustic fritters sold along the street to refined lobster dishes found in the country's leading restaurants.

Haiti is world famous for its delicious, spice-laden foods such as rice and beans, *griyo* and *pen patat*. *Town and Country* brings these delicacies into your home – no matter where you live. We have included an assortment of traditional and modern Haitian Creole and French-influenced recipes, as well as selections from famous Haitian restaurants, all using the abundant selection of vegetables, meats, and tropical fruits found in Haiti.

Our straightforward directions and simple format make your cooking experience as easy as possible, while striving to maintain the authenticity of Haitian cuisine. *Town and Country* is loaded with extras and variations that make it a cook-friendly recipe collection.

We have provided tips on cooking with Haitian flavors and the uses of unique ingredients, along with charts that tell you the names of foods in French, Creole, and English. Be sure to watch for the added seasoning of Haitian proverbs sprinkled throughout the book – they show great wisdom and a delightful sense of humor.

We trust your experience with *Town and Country* will be complete with a generous appetite, a crowded table, and, above all, excellent food.

Bon Appétit!

This book is dedicated to Gilliane Angus who cooks with recipes from her heart and adds the not-so-secret ingredient of love to everything she does.

TABLE OF CONTENTS

PICKLED CONCH (LAMBI)

1 lb. conch, cleaned and peeled	2 Habanero peppers
1 c. white vinegar	1 medium onion sliced
3 cloves garlic crushed	12 whole cloves
1 tsp. allspice	½ tsp. salt

Pound the conch well with a wooden mallet. In a heavy sauce pan, bring several cups of salted water to a brisk boil. Drop the conch into the boiling water and cook 3 to 5 minutes until tender. The conch becomes tough and loses its succulence if overcooked. Reserve one cup of the broth. Drain well and cut the conch into bite size pieces.

Combine the reserved broth with the rest of the ingredients to make a marinade for the conch. Cover the conch with marinade and refrigerate for twenty-four hours. If a spicier dish is desired, increase the number of Habanero peppers to taste.

Serve with crackers.

CODFISH SALAD HORS D'OEUVRE (CHIKTAY)

1 lb. dried salted codfish	1 c. shredded red cabbage
¾ c. olive oil	1 c. shredded green cabbage
¾ c. white wine vinegar	1 medium yellow onion, diced
½ c. chopped fresh parsley	1 medium red onion, diced
½ c. carrots, shredded	½ c. scallions, sliced
	6 Habanero peppers, seeds removed and diced

Soak the codfish for 24 hours, changing the water several times. Boil the fish until it is tender but not mushy (10-20 minutes). Shred the fish with a fork into half inch pieces.

Mix all the ingredients together into a non-metallic container and let stand in the refrigerator for at least one hour. Turn the ingredients over once or twice.

Serve on crackers or lightly toasted slices of baguette.

Malanga Akra Fritters

1 c. malanga, grated	salt and pepper to taste
1 tsp. parsley, chopped fine	cooking oil
½ Habanero pepper	

Carefully remove the seeds from the Habanero pepper (See Index, How to Handle Chilies). Chop half of the Habanero pepper into small bits. Combine together the malanga, parsley, pepper and seasonings. At this point the mixture can be kept in the refrigerator for several hours or freezer until ready to use. When ready to use, heat cooking oil. Drop batter by 1 tablespoon into oil and deep-fry until golden in color.

Meat Pie (Pate)

2 c. flour	1 Tbs. shortening
½ c. butter	4 Tbs. water
pinch of salt	Filling (see below)

Mix all ingredients together (except filling). Place dough on a floured surface and begin rolling it into a rectangle, about ¼" thick. Cut dough into squares. Place a small amount of filling on one half of the square. Bring the other side over filling to form a triangle. Close the edges by pressing a fork along the edges. If dough does not stick to itself, wet edges with a small amount of water then press again. Prick the top with a fork to allow steam to escape. Bake at 350 degrees until tops of pies are golden brown (about 20-30 minutes).

Filling

1 lb. ground beef	1 Tbs. tomato paste
1 clove garlic, crushed	½ c. onion, finely chopped
pinch of salt	½ tsp. thyme

Brown the ground beef in skillet. Drain off excess fat. Add other ingredients, stirring on low heat until mixed thoroughly.

Chicken may be substituted for the ground beef. Shread 1 lb. cooked chicken and proceed with other ingredients.

MARINAD FRITTERS

1 ¼ c. flour	1 large clove garlic, crushed
1 c. water	1 tsp. baking powder
¼ c. onion	½ tsp. baking soda
¼ c. parsley, chopped	¼ tsp. salt
½ tsp. Habanero pepper sauce (or other hot sauce)	cooking oil

Grind the onion, parsley and garlic in a mortar or blend it with water in a blender to extract the maximum flavor. Add the dry ingredients and mix into a sticky batter. Batter should be too sticky to form by hand but runny enough to drop off a spoon.

Drop the batter by small spoonfuls into 350 degree oil and fry until golden on both sides. Serve with hot pickliz relish (See Index).

NOTE: Oil temperature is critical. If it is too low the fritters will be greasy and if it is too hot, the centers will not be cooked.

Variations: For added flavor, marinads frequently include bits of shredded dried **codfish** or **herring** that has been soaked and washed to reduce saltiness.

Conch (Lambi) may also be added. Boil the conch in slightly salted water and chop fine.

PINEAPPLE NOG

1 can pineapple, crushed	½ c. coconut milk
4 eggs	1 c. milk
$1/_8$ tsp. nutmeg	

Combine ingredients in blender and blend well. Top drink with additional nutmeg. Fresh pineapple may be used instead of canned.

Spicy Cocoa

3 unbeaten egg whites	4 to 6 Tbs. sugar
¾ c. cocoa	1 c. cold milk
1 tsp. cinnamon, powdered	11 c. milk

Mix into a paste the eggs whites, cocoa, cinnamon and sugar. Dilute the paste with the cold milk. Boil the 11 cups of milk over low heat. Add the paste gradually to the milk, beating constantly. Serve hot and foamy.

Limeade (Sitwonad)

For each cup of water, add

1½ Tbs. lime juice	3-4 Tbs. sugar
⅛ tsp. salt	

The sugar and water need not be boiled, but the quality of the limeade is improved if they are. Boil the sugar and water for 2 minutes. Chill the syrup and add the lime juice.

Suggestion: Sometimes a small amount of vanilla is added. For each gallon of juice add about ¼ teaspoon of vanilla (add to taste).

Corn Pudding (Akasan, AK-100)

1 c. corn flour	2 star anise
¼ c. sugar	1 tsp. vanilla extract
1 can (12 oz) evaporated milk	¼ tsp. salt
2 sticks cinnamon	

Stir the corn flour in a cup of cold water and let stand for 5 minutes. Bring 4 cups of water to a boil. Add the cinnamon, star anise and salt. Boil 5 minutes.

Slowly pour the dissolved corn flour into the boiling water with constant stirring. Cook until the mixture thickens – about 5 minutes. Remove from heat. Remove cinnamon and star anise. Add evaporated milk and vanilla.

Serve as a thick drink with milk and sugar to desired consistency.

FRESH TOMATO JUICE

12 medium ripe tomatoes
½ c. water
1 slice onion
1 rib celery with leaves
 salt to taste

½ bay leaf
2 sprigs parsley
¼ tsp. paprika
¼ tsp. sugar

Simmer tomatoes with water, onion, celery, bay leaf and parsley for ½ hour. Strain juice and season with salt, paprika, and sugar. Serve thoroughly chilled.

MANGO JUICE

4 c. water or 3 bottles of
 soda water
 juice of 12 oranges

2 mangoes (francique variety)
1 c. sugar

Boil sugar and water together until sugar is dissolved, let mixture cool. Purée mango meat and orange juice in blender. Add sugar water with puree and blend well. Pour into pitcher filled with ice cubes and serve.

SOURSOP JUICE (JI KOWOSÒL)

2 c. soursop pulp (1 med.)
2 c. water
 nutmeg (optional)

1 qt. milk
 sugar to taste

Blend soursop pulp and water together first, then add the milk and sweeten. Blend until smooth. (Add crushed ice to get a slushy effect.) Chill.

Haitian Proverb: If you planted cassava
you can't harvest sweet potatoes.

(You reap what you sow.)

BASIC CREOLE SAUCE

Serves 4

1 or 2 onions
¼ lb. lean diced bacon
2 tomatoes, peeled,
seeded and diced

2 c. watercress
2 c. water
salt and pepper to taste

Slice onions very thin and sauté in butter or oil with tomatoes and bacon. Wash, dry and strip leaves of watercress and add into pan. When the watercress is wilted, add water, salt and pepper and allow to simmer 15 minutes.

VERY EASY TOMATO SAUCE

2 Tbs. butter
2 Tbs. flour

1 small tin tomato paste
1 c. cold water

Melt butter and add flour. Stir well. Mix water and tomato paste together and add to flour mixture. Stir over heat until thick.

BEAN SAUCE (SÒS PWA)

1 c. dried red beans
4 c. water
8 whole cloves
1 large clove garlic, crushed

1 tsp. fresh thyme
salt and pepper to taste
1 tsp. oil

(For a **Quick and Easy** version, substitute canned red beans and reduce water to 1 cup.)

Cover beans with water and soak overnight or for several hours. Drain. Put oil in sauce pan. Heat. Add drained beans and sauté quickly with garlic, cloves and thyme. Add 4 cups water and cook until beans are tender. Remove ¼ cup whole beans. Blend or purée remaining beans and liquid. Add whole beans. Simmer, stirring to avoid sticking, until consistency of thick gravy. Dumplings or Bòy may be added. (See Index) Continue simmering until dumplings are cooked.

MORNAY SAUCE (CHEESE SAUCE)

Great with fish, shellfish or chicken

¾ c. white wine
¾ c. water from poached
   fish or chicken broth
½ tsp. white pepper
1 c. cream or half and half
½ tsp. fresh thyme

1 tsp. fresh parsley
1 c. grated Swiss cheese

4 Tbs. butter or butter
3 Tbs. flour
  salt to taste

In blender or food processor, mix ¼ cup of wine with the thyme and parsley, purée. In saucepan, melt the butter and add the flour stirring to make a paste. Gradually add the broth/water, wine and thyme mixture, stirring to avoid lumps. Add the pepper and salt. Stir in the cheese, reserving ¼ cup for sprinkling on top of dish. Pour over fish or meat, sprinkle with remaining cheese and bake in oven until cooked.

EASY MORNAY SAUCE (CHEESE SAUCE)

4 Tbs. butter
4 Tbs. flour
2 c. hot milk

3 egg yolks
½ c. cheese, grated

Melt butter in saucepan. Add in flour and stir 3 or 4 minutes until sauce is smooth. Then add milk, stirring constantly. While still stirring, add in egg yolks. Remove from heat and fold in cheese.

NEVER-FAIL HOLLANDAISE SAUCE

4 egg yolks	pinch cayenne
1 c. butter or butter, melted	2 Tbs. lime juice
½ tsp. salt	

Over low heat, melt butter or butter and allow to cool. Beat egg yolks until thick and lemon-colored. Add salt and cayenne. Gradually add melted butter, while beating briskly by hand, or on high speed in electric beater, blending each addition well before the next. Alternate with teaspoonfuls of lime juice and continue until smooth.

SHALLOT SAUCE

(Easy sauce to accompany fish or rice dish)

1 c. shallots, thinly sliced	½ tsp. course salt
½ c. olive oil	¼ c. white wine vinegar

Mix ingredients together about an hour before use. This makes an excellent sauce for fish (see Pwason Gwo Sèl) and rice dishes (see Diri ak Pwa). Sauce may be stored in the refrigerator for several days.

BÉCHAMEL SAUCE

$^1/_8$ c. carrots, chopped	2 Tbs. butter
¼ c. onions, chopped	3 Tbs. flour
chopped herbs	1½ c. hot milk
¼ c. bacon or ham diced	
(optional)	

Sauté carrots and onions 15 minutes in butter with or without bacon or ham. Remove from butter. Add flour to butter, then the hot milk, stirring constantly. Return vegetables and bacon or ham, season to taste and allow to simmer 45 minutes. Put the sauce through sieve and correct seasonings as needed. Serve with fish, shell-fish, vegetables, etc.

MARINADES (FOR BARBECUE)

Meat:

½ c. vinegar
¼ c. lime or lemon juice
½ c. oil
1 clove garlic, crushed

½ tsp. salt
pinch black pepper
small bay leaf, crushed

Poultry:

1 c. tomato sauce
½ c. butter
2 Tbs. onion, chopped fine

¼ c. lime or lemon juice
1 tsp. salt
1 Tbs. Worcestershire sauce

Fish:

1 c. lime or lemon juice
½ c. oil
1 clove garlic
½ tsp. salt

1 tsp. Worcestershire sauce
1 bay leaf, crushed
pinch black pepper
pinch tarragon

Allow to stand half an hour or more in marinade. Drain, barbecue, basting with marinade.

PEPPERCORN SAUCE

2-4 Tbs. peppercorns, ground
½ c. unsalted butter, cut into
small pieces

1 c. whipping cream
(or canned cream)

Sauté peppercorns in small amount of butter; add cream and stir well, add remaining butter. Taste and adjust seasoning. Pour over meat.

GOLDEN PAPAYA BASTE

9 oz. fresh papaya, mashed
¼ tsp. ginger powdered
1 Tbs. honey
2 Tbs. white vinegar or fruit
    juice

2 Tbs. salad oil
2 Tbs. butter, melted
¼ tsp. salt

Combine all ingredients. Simmer 10-15 minutes. Use to coat chicken or pork before baking in oven.

SWEET AND SOUR SAUCE

½ c. white vinegar
½ c. white sugar
½ c. water

2 tsp. cornstarch
$1/_8$ c. soy sauce
½ c. pineapple, crushed

Combine the vinegar and sugar. Cook over medium heat until sugar is dissolved. Mix the cornstarch into the water and soy sauce. Add this, plus the pineapple to the sugar mixture. Boil until mixture becomes transparent and thick. Serve warm or cold.

TI MALICE SAUCE

½ c. shallots, thinly sliced
¼ c. white vinegar
1 c. olive oil

½ tsp. coarse salt
1 Habanero pepper

Carefully, cut the Habanero pepper in half. Remove seeds without touching them. Chop the pepper into tiny bits. Mix with rest of ingredients. Let stand or chill for at least 4 hours before serving. Is an excellent accompaniment to fish dishes.

Variation: For an even hotter sauce, add a few of the Habanero seeds to the mixture.

Breads and Rolls

CASSAVA BREAD (KASAV)

2 medium to large yuca (manyòk)   salt

Peel, rinse, and grate the yuca roots. (If using bitter yuca, rinse the grated pulp several times before pressing.) Add a little salt. Place the grated yuca in a clean dish towel. Roll the towel and by twisting the ends in opposite directions, squeeze hard to eliminate as much juice from the yuca as possible. Heat a griddle and sprinkle yucca onto griddle in a circular pattern, about 1/8 inch thick. Press down with spatula. (A metal hoop may be used for even edges.) Cook over moderate heat until bread is set. Turn and cook on other side until crisp.

NOTE: Cassava bread can be easily refreshed by lightly toasting. Toasted cassava bread with butter or spicy peanut butter (See Index) makes a great snack.

BRIOCHE

Makes 24 rolls

1 pkg. active dry yeast   3½ c. flour
½ c. butter   ½ c. milk
⅓ c. sugar   4 eggs
½ tsp. salt   1 Tbs. sugar

Soften yeast in ¼ c. warm water. Cream butter, ⅓ c. sugar, and salt. Add 1 c. of flour and the milk to creamed mixture. Beat 3 eggs and 1 egg yolk together (reserve egg whites). Add softened yeast and eggs to creamed mixture; beat well. Add remaining flour. By hand, beat for 5 to 8 minutes. Cover; let rise in warm place until doubled (about 2 hours). Stir down, beat well, cover, and refrigerate overnight.

Stir down and turn out onto floured surface. Set aside ¼ of dough. Cut remaining dough into 24 equal pieces. With floured hands, shape into balls and put into greased muffin pans. Cut reserved dough into 24 equal pieces and shape into balls.

Make an indentation in each large ball. Brush with water and press small balls into indentations. Cover; let rise until doubled (about 30 minutes). Combine 1 slightly beaten egg white and 1 Tbs. sugar; brush tops. Bake at 375 degrees about 15 minutes.

Coconut Bread

Makes 3 small loaves

1 Tbs. butter softened plus 4
    Tbs. butter melted

5 c. plus 3 Tbs. flour
2 c. sugar
1 Tbs. double-acting baking
    powder
¾ tsp. salt

1 lg. coconut opened,
    peeled and finely
    grated
2 c. milk
¼ tsp. ground cloves
½ tsp. ground cinnamon

Preheat the oven to 350 degrees. With a pastry brush, spread 1 Tbs. of softened butter evenly over the bottom and sides of three 3 ½ x 7 inch loaf pans. Sprinkle 1 Tbs. of the flour into each pan and tip the pans from side to side to spread it evenly. Then invert the pans and rap the bottom sharply to remove any excess flour. Set aside.

Sift the remaining 5 cups of flour, the sugar, baking powder, cinnamon, cloves and salt into a deep bowl. Add the grated coconut and with your hands or a large spoon, mix all the ingredients together well. Pour in the milk, ½ cup at a time, and blend thoroughly after each addition. Then stir in the 4 Tbs. of melted butter.

Ladle the coconut batter into the prepared pans, filling each of them no more than two thirds full. Bake the bread in the middle of the oven for 1 hour, or until it begins to pull away from the sides of the pans and the top is golden brown and crusty. Remove the bread from the oven and let it cool in the pans for about 5 minutes, then turn the loaves out onto wire cake racks. Serve the coconut bread either warm or cool.

NOTE: Four cups of packaged grated coconut or frozen flaked coconut may be substituted for the freshly grated coconut. If the prepared coconut is pre-sweetened (most brands are), reduce the amount of sugar in the recipe from 2 cups to 1½ cups. If you want to reduce the size of the packaged flakes to make the bread less crunchy, pulvarise the coconut in a food processor for a few seconds.

CORN BREAD

2 Tbs. melted butter	½ tsp. salt
1 c. flour	3 tsp. baking powder
¾ c. corn meal	1 egg
1½ Tbs. sugar	1 c. milk

Melt butter in a shallow pan, about 10" x 14". Sift flour, corn meal, sugar, salt and baking powder together into a large bowl. Beat egg in smaller bowl, add milk, then melted butter and gradually pour mixture into dry ingredients, mixing without beating, until well blended. Add a little more butter to pan, which should still be hot. Pour in batter and bake 25 to 30 minutes in hot oven (425 degrees).

EASY FRENCH BREAD

Makes 2 loaves

2 packages dry yeast	2 c. boiling water
½ c. warm water	7 ½ 8 c. flour
2 Tbs. sugar	1 egg, beaten
2 tsp. salt	2 Tbs. milk
2 Tbs. shortening	poppy or sesame seeds

Dissolve yeast in warm water. Combine sugar, shortening, salt, and water together and let cool to lukewarm. Add in yeast mixture. Stir in flour.

Knead 10 minutes, or until smooth and elastic. Place in greased bowl, turning once. Let rise until doubled. Punch down and let rest 15 minutes. Divide dough in half. On floured surface, roll each half to a 12" x 15" rectangle. Roll up, starting at 15" edge. Place loaves on greased cookie sheets and make 4 or 5 slashes diagonally across tops. Let rise until double.

Mix egg and milk and brush on top of bread. Sprinkle on poppy or sesame seeds, if desired. Bake 400 degrees for 20 minutes.

RAISIN BREAD

Makes 1 loaf

½ c. sugar
1 Tbs. salt
3 Tbs. shortening
1 egg

3 c. warm water
2 Tbs. yeast
5-6 c. flour
½ c. raisins

Dissolve yeast into ½ cup warm water. Let stand in a warm place for about 10 minutes. Beat in the sugar, salt, shortening, egg, raisins, and the rest of the water. Sift the flour and begin mixing it into the rest of the ingredients. Knead, shape into ball and allow to rise in oiled bowl until it has doubled in size. Punch down and shape into greased loaf pan and allow mixture to rise again. To bake, place loaf pan in a cold oven. Turn the heat to 400 degrees. After 15 minutes, reduce heat to 375 degrees and bake 25 minutes more. Remove the loaf at once from the pan and cool on a rack before storing.

ZUCCHINI BREAD

Makes 3 loaves

4 c. flour
½ tsp. salt
¼ tsp. baking powder
1 tsp. baking soda
2 tsp. cinnamon
1 Tbs. ground cloves

3 eggs
1 c. oil
3 tsp. vanilla
2 c. brown sugar
3 c. zucchini, grated

Sift first six ingredients together. Beat eggs and add to the remaining ingredients. Mix flour mixture with zucchini mixture and pour into greased loaf pans. Bake at 350 degrees for 1 hour.

PUMPKIN BREAD

Makes 2 loaves

1 c. milk	½ tsp. ginger
1 c. pumpkin, pureed	2 Tbs. baking powder
¼ c. sugar	6 ½ c. flour
2 eggs	1 tsp. salt
½ c. warm water	1 tsp. cinnamon
¼ c. butter	

Mix together milk, pureed pumpkin, butter, sugar, warm water, and eggs. Sift together the dry ingredients and mix in with the liquid mixture. Pour into greased loaf pans and cook for 1 hour at 350 degrees.

WHITE BREAD

Makes 4 loaves

2 packages dry yeast	½ c. sugar
½ c. warm water	¼ c. butter or shortening
1 tsp. sugar	3 c. warm water
2 tsp. salt	11 c. flour

Dissolve yeast in warm water and 1 tsp. sugar. Combine salt, shortening, ½ cup sugar, water and yeast mixture in large mixing bowl. Mix well. Add 5 c. flour and beat with electric mixer for 3 minutes. Stir in 6 c. flour by hand.

Turn onto floured board and knead 5 minutes. Place in greased bowl, turning once, cover and let rise ½ hour. Punch down, turn over and let rise again until doubled. Knead a few minutes, then shape into 4 loaves and place in greased 9" x 5" loaf pans. Cover loaves with damp cloth and let rise until doubled. Bake at 350 degrees for 30 - 35 minutes. Brush tops with butter if desired.

BANANA BREAD

Makes one 9" x 5" x 3" loaf

9 Tbs. butter, softened
¼ c. seedless raisins
2 c. all purpose flour
1 Tbs. baking powder
1 egg
¼ tsp. ground nutmeg,
    preferably fresh

¼ tsp. salt
2 large ripe bananas (1 lb.)
1 tsp. vanilla extract
½ c. sugar
¾ c. unsalted nuts(optional)

Preheat oven to 350 degrees.

Reserve ¼ cup of the most perfectly shaped nuts for the garnish. Chop the rest of the nuts coarsely and toss them with the raisins and 1 Tbs. of the flour. Sift the remaining flour with the baking powder, nutmeg and salt.

In a small bowl, mash the bananas to a smooth puree. Stir in the vanilla and set aside.

In a deep bowl, cream the remaining butter and the sugar together.

Add the egg, and when it is well blended beat in the flour and the bananas alternately, adding about one third of each mixture at a time, and continue to beat until the batter is smooth. Gently but thoroughly stir in the chopped nuts and raisins.

Pour batter into a greased loaf pan and arrange the reserved nuts attractively on the top. Bake the bread in the middle of the oven for 50 to 60 minutes, or until a toothpick inserted into the center of the loaf comes out clean. Remove the bread from the oven and let it cool in the pan for 5 minutes, then turn it out on a wire cake rack. Serve the banana bread either warm or cool.

CROISSANTS (KWASAN)

Makes about 18

All ingredients should be room temperature.

$7/_8$ c. milk	$1/_3$ c. lukewarm water
1½ Tbs. sugar	2½ c. flour, sifted
¾ tsp. salt	1 c. + 1 Tbl butter, softened
1 pkg yeast	

Scald milk; add 1 Tbl butter, sugar and salt. Cool until lukewarm. Dissolve yeast in water then add to milk mixture. Stir in or knead in flour to make a soft dough.

Knead dough on a lightly floured surface until smooth and elastic. Place in a greased bowl and turn so all sides are lightly greased. Cover with a damp cloth. Let rise until doubled in bulk, about 1½ hours. Cover the dough with a lid and chill thoroughly, at least 20 minutes.

Roll dough out into an oblong ¼" thick.

Beat remaining butter until creamy. Dot $2/_3$ of the surface of the dough with ¼ c. of the butter. Fold the undotted third over the center third. Then, fold the doubled portion over the remaining third of the butter-dotted portion. The dough is now 3 layers thick. Turn the layered dough a ¼ turn and repeat again. Do this two more times, making it a total of four times that you roll it and fold it. Cover and chill at least 2 hours. Then roll the dough again on a floured surface. Cut the dough into 3" squares. Cut the squares in half diagonally. Roll the triangular pieces beginning with the wide side and stretching it slightly as you roll. Shape the rolls into crescents. Place on a baking sheet and chill for ½ hour. Preheat oven to 400 degrees and bake for 10 minutes, then reduce the heat to 350 degrees and bake them for about 10 to 15 minutes longer or until done.

MOCK APPLE MUFFINS

Makes 12 muffins

1 ¾ c. flour	¼ tsp. lime juice
¼ c. sugar	¾ c. milk
2½ tsp. baking powder	⅓ c. cooking oil
¾ tsp. salt	1 c. peeled & chopped militon
½ tsp. ground cinnamon	2½ Tbs. sugar
1 well-beaten egg	½ tsp. ground cinnamon

Stir thoroughly first 5 ingredients; make a well in the center. Blend egg, lime juice, milk, oil, and militon; add all at once to dry mixture. Stir just until moistened. Fill greased muffin pans ⅔ full. Sprinkle with mixture of 2½ Tbs. sugar and ½ tsp. cinnamon. Bake at 400 degrees about 20 minutes.

Variation: For "Apricot" muffins: Use 1 c. peeled tropical apricots; remove white layer between skin and fruit; boil in water for about 5 minutes. If apricot is sour, add sugar to taste. Omit lime juice.

TROPICAL MUFFINS

Makes 18 muffins

2 c. all-purpose flour	1 c. dairy sour cream
2 tsp. baking powder	8¾ oz. can crushed pineapple
½ tsp. baking soda	½ c. chopped nuts
½ tsp. salt	⅓ c. cooking oil
½ c. packed brown sugar	¼ c. coconut
1 well-beaten egg	

Stir together thoroughly the flour, baking powder, baking soda, salt; stir in brown sugar. Combine egg and sour cream. Stir in undrained pineapple, nuts, oil, and coconut; add to dry ingredients all at once. Stir until moistened. Fill greased muffin pans ⅔ full. Bake at 400 degrees about 20 minutes.

FRENCH DOUGHNUTS - BEIGNETS
Makes 36

3 c. all-purpose flour	¼ c. sugar
1 pkg. active dry yeast	¼ c. cooking oil
½ tsp. ground nutmeg	1 egg
1 c. milk	powdered sugar
$2/3$ tsp. salt	

Combine 1½ c. flour, yeast, and nutmeg. In saucepan heat milk, sugar, oil, and salt just until warm. (115-120 degrees). Add to dry mixture; add egg. Beat at low speed with mixer for ½ minute, scraping bowl. Beat 3 minutes at high speed. Stir in enough remaining flour to make a soft dough. Place in greased bowl; turn once. Cover and chill.

Turn dough out on well floured surface; form into ball. Cover; let rest 10 minutes. Roll to 18" x 12" rectangle. Cut in 3" x 2" rectangles. Cover; let rise (30 minutes) - dough will not be doubled. Fry in deep hot fat (375 degrees), turning once, until golden, about 1 minute. Drain. Dip in powdered sugar.

DATE - ORANGE COFFEE CAKE

2 c. all-purpose flour	1 tsp. ground cinnamon
½ c. granulated sugar	3 tsp. grated orange peel
3 tsp. baking powder	$2/3$ c. orange juice
1 slightly beaten egg	½ c. chopped nuts
½ c. cooking oil	½ c. brown sugar
½ c. milk	3 Tbs. butter, soft
½ tsp. salt	½ c. snipped dates (or use prunes; raisins)

Stir the first 3 ingredients together with ½ tsp. salt. Combine egg, milk, and oil; add all at once to dry ingredients. Stir just until well mixed. Combine dates, peel, and juice; stir into batter just until blended. Spread evenly in greased baking pan. Mix remaining ingredients; sprinkle over batter. Bake at 375 degrees for 25 to 30 minutes.

CINNAMON ROLLS

Makes 24

3½ - 4 c. all-purpose flour	2 eggs
1 pkg. dry yeast	$1/3$ c. butter, melted
1 c. milk	$2/3$ c. sugar
¼ c. sugar	3 tsp. cinnamon
¼ c. shortening	¾ c. raisins
1 tsp. salt	confectioner's icing (see below)

In large mixer bowl combine 2 c. flour and yeast. Heat milk, ¼ c. sugar, ¼ c. shortening, and salt in saucepan until warm (115-120 degrees), stirring to melt shortening. Add to dry mixture; add eggs. Beat at low speed with electric mixer for ½ minute, scraping bowl. Beat 3 minutes at high speed by hand, stir in 1½ to 2 c. flour to make a moderately stiff dough. Knead on lightly floured surface until smooth. Shape into a ball. Place in greased bowl, turning once. Cover; let rise until doubled (45 to 60 minutes). Punch down; divide in half. Cover; let rest 10 minutes.

Roll each half of dough into 12" x 8" rectangle. Brush each with half of the melted butter. Combine sugar and cinnamon; sprinkle over dough. Sprinkle with raisins, if desired. Roll up each piece, starting with long side; seal seams. Slice each into 12 rolls. Place rolls, cut side down, in two greased 9" x 1½" round baking pans. Cover and let rise until doubled (about 35 minutes). Bake at 375 degrees for 18 to 20 minutes. Drizzle icing over warm rolls.

Confectioner's Icing:

1 c. sifted powdered sugar	¼ tsp. vanilla
1½ Tbs. milk	

Combine sugar, vanilla, and milk. Drizzle icing over cooled rolls. Add nuts or fruits on top of icing before it sets if desired.

SALADS AND SOUPS

BOUYON SOUP

3 yellow sweet potatoes	2 c. string beans
2 green plantains	1 c. watercress
2 medium white potatoes	1 c. okra, sliced
1 malanga	1 green pepper, sliced
3 medium carrots	2 onions-sliced
salt and pepper	

Boil watercress, onion, and okra in 2 quarts of water until okra becomes stringy. Cut sweet potatoes, plantains, malanga, and carrots into quarters and add with 1 Tbs. salt. Boil until half cooked. Then add white potatoes, green pepper, and string beans. Soup should become thick. Add salt and pepper to taste. Dumplings or bòy may be added. (See Index) Continue simmering until dumplings are cooked.

CONCH (LAMBI) CHOWDER

Serves 6

1¹/₃ c. onion, chopped	sherry and Tabasco to taste
¾ c. celery, chopped	1½ tsp. each oregano, salt, thyme
2 tsp. garlic, minced	½ tsp. each cayenne and black pepper
¼ c. bacon fat	2 c. potatoes, peeled, diced
1 lb. conch, ground	28 oz. tomatoes with liquid
5 c. water	½ c. onions, chopped
3 Tbs. tomato paste	¾ c. carrots, diced

In a large stainless or enameled saucepan cook the onion, celery and garlic in bacon fat over moderate heat for ten minutes. Add 1 lb. ground conch and cook another 10 minutes. Add water, tomatoes, plus juice, tomato paste, oregano, salt and thyme, cayenne and black pepper and simmer for approximately 45 minutes. Add 2 cups potatoes and carrots and simmer for 15 minutes. If necessary add one more cup water to dilute to desired consistency. Add salt to taste and if desired 1 Tbs. dry sherry and Tabasco.

PUMPKIN SOUP (SOUP JOUMOU)

Traditionally in Haiti, this soup is the first food to be eaten on New Years Day - to bring you good luck.

1 lb. beef stew meat	1 lb. joumou (pumpkin)
1 lb. chicken	¼ c. celery stalk and leaves
½ lb. cabbage	2 large carrots
1 onion	3 med. potatoes
3 cloves	¼ qt. water
3 medium sized turnips	1 Tbs. lemon or lime juice
1 hot pimento, whole with stem	¼ lb. vermicelli or pasta

Use a large kettle to boil the beef and the chicken with the lime juice and cloves for about 20 minutes. Remove any froth that formed. Add all the vegetables. Continue boiling until meat is tender and vegetables are cooked (35 - 40 minutes.) Turn off the heat and let cool. Cube the meat and strain the vegetables through a fine sieve. Return cubed meat and liquid to kettle and bring to boil. Add the whole pimiento, being careful not to break or puncture it. (It is added more for aroma than flavor). Add the vermicelli or pasta and simmer until vermicelli is cooked. Add dumplings or bòy (See Index) if desired and continue to simmer until dumplings are cooked.

GARLIC SOUP

Serves 6

12 to 18 cloves garlic	1 c. olive oil
sprig of thyme	1 egg
1½ qt. water or broth	salt and pepper
stale bread	dash vinegar

Boil garlic and thyme 20 minutes in water or broth. Beat egg at high speed adding oil in a slow steady stream. Warm egg mixture with 2-3 tablespoons of hot soup and then add it to the soup. Add vinegar, salt and pepper. Serve over stale or toasted bread.

CONCH (LAMBI) SOUP

1 lb. conch	1 tomato, peeled
2 Tbs. lime juice	sprig of fresh basil
1½ qt. chicken broth	½ c. carrots, diced
1 clove garlic, slivered	salt and pepper
1 green pepper, sliced	1 c. uncooked vermicelli
1 onion, sliced	4 or 6 drops Tabasco sauce

Wash and trim conch. Dry the conch thoroughly, then pound it with floured wooden mallet. Rub it with lime juice. Cut conch into bite-size pieces and set aside for later use. In a heavy kettle bring to a brisk boil broth, tomato, onion, green pepper, garlic, and basil. Reduce heat and simmer for about twenty minutes. Remove broth from fire and strain, discarding vegetables. Return broth to the fire and add carrots. Simmer for about twenty minutes. Add to broth the conch, pepper, salt, vermicelli and Tabasco sauce. Simmer an additional ten minutes, or just until the conch is tender. Do not overcook. Serve hot.

CREAMED LEEK AND POTATO SOUP

Serves 6

3 medium leeks	4 c. chicken stock
1 medium onion, chopped	1- 2 c. cream
2 Tbs. butter	salt and pepper to taste
4 medium potatoes, peeled and sliced very thin	chopped watercress or chives

Mince the white parts of leeks and sauté with onions for 3 minutes in butter. Add potatoes and chicken stock. Simmer covered for 15 minutes or until vegetables are tender. Put through food mill or blender. Add cream and spices. Heat thoroughly and serve. Decorate with watercress or chives.

Serve hot or very cold. Soup should be reduced to a velvety smoothness.

GREEN PLANTAIN SOUP

1 lb. salted beef	2 scallions
4 c. fresh water	2 tsp. Worcestershire sauce
1 clove garlic	1 Tbs. tomato paste
Few sprigs parsley	½ c. chopped celery
1½ c. shredded cabbage	2 very green plantains
2 celery stalks, with leaves	1 bay leaf, slightly crushed
¾ tsp. salt	1 cinnamon stick

Place the beef in a heavy kettle with water, garlic, parsley, celery stalks, scallions, bay leaf and salt; bring to a brisk boil. Reduce heat and simmer until meat is tender. Strain broth, discarding the vegetables. Dice the beef and set aside. Return the broth to the fire and bring again to a gentle boil. Add to the broth Worcestershire sauce, tomato paste, and chopped celery.

Slice plantains into thick rounds and fry in two or three Tbs. butter until golden. Pound each round with a wooden mallet until flat, and add immediately to the soup. Simmer an additional fifteen minutes.

During the last few minutes of cooking time add cabbage, diced beef and cinnamon stick. Discard cinnamon stick before serving the soup.

Haitian Proverb: Among the grains of rice the pebble tastes the grease.

(Without you, I'd never be where I am.
Thanks to you I'm sharing this blessing.)

KIDNEY BEAN SOUP (SOUP PWA WOUJ)

1 lb. kidney beans	1 Tbs. chopped cilantro
6 slices bacon	½ tsp. fresh thyme
4 c. water	¼ tsp. black pepper
4 c. chicken stock	1 tsp. salt
1 medium onion, diced	4 cloves
1 Tbs. chopped parsley	

In a large Dutch oven or pot, dice the bacon and fry it to render the fat. Add all the remaining ingredients except the liquids and stir for 30 seconds. Add the water and chicken stock and bring to a boil. Add the beans and return to a boil. Cook until the beans are very tender. Add water if necessary. When beans are tender, purée and strain the soup. Add liquid if necessary for a thick but not pasty consistency. Serve hot with a dollop of crème fraîche and hot pepper sauce to taste.

Variation: For a vegetarian version, omit bacon and substitute with 1 teaspoon olive oil. Use vegetable stock instead of chicken stock.

For a quick and easy version, use canned kidney beans. Replace 1 lb. of beans with 3 cans of beans. Drain and rinse before using.

Haitian Proverb: The big water pot is not a spring.

(Conserve your resources or they will run out.)

ONION SOUP GRATINÉE

4 c. white onions, sliced thin
4 Tbs. olive oil
2 c. beef consommé
1 c. water
¼ tsp. white pepper
2 c. red wine
French bread slices
Gruyere cheese (1 oz per serving)

The trick to good onion soup is in the preparation of the onions. Slice the onions into thin rounds and separate pieces. Sauté the onions in oil and cook until they become translucent and just start to take color. Remove from heat when just a few of the onions begin to turn light brown.

Put the water and consommé in a deep pan and add the onions. Bring to a boil and add 1 ½ cups of the red wine. Reduce heat and simmer at least 30 minutes. (This can be put into a crock pot and allowed to cook several hours or all day.) Shortly before serving, add the remaining ½ cup red wine. Let the mixture come to a boil and then remove from heat.

Put into individual ovenproof bowls. Press one ounce of grated cheese onto a lightly toasted piece of French bread. Float on top of soup. Place bowls on a cookie sheet and put into a hot oven (400 degrees). Bake until cheese on top has melted and turned golden.

Haitian Proverb: The good dumpling does not float.

(Good things are not easy. Good people are hard to find.)

RICH CHICKEN SOUP

Serves 6

2½ lb. chicken legs
1 medium onion, minced
1 small green pepper, chopped
2 stalks celery, chopped with leaves
3 potatoes, peeled and quartered
2 medium tomatoes, peeled
¼ tsp. nutmeg
1 tsp. cumin
1 tsp. poultry seasoning
½ tsp. Italian season
salt and pepper
2 carrots, cut into thick diagonal slices
½ fresh pumpkin, peeled, cut in serving pieces
2 firm green plantains, sliced thick rounds
2 white yams, quartered
3 shallots, minced
½ small cabbage, shredded

Rub chicken with lime juice. Chop the peeled tomatoes. Make a marinade out of the onion, green pepper, celery, shallots, tomatoes, poultry seasoning, nutmeg, cumin, Italian seasoning, salt and pepper. Mix with the chicken and refrigerate for twenty-four hours. Scrape the marinade from the chicken legs. Simmer marinade in a large kettle for ten minutes. Add the chicken legs and enough water to cover. Bring to a boil, reduce heat and simmer until chicken is tender, about 30 - 40 minutes. Skim the surface of the broth as foam appears. Remove the chicken and strain the broth, discarding the vegetables.

Return the broth to the kettle and add carrots and pumpkin. Cook for 10 minutes. Next add plantains and yams and cook for 20 minutes more. Then add cabbage and cook for 5 more minutes. Return the chicken to the kettle and heat thoroughly.

KIDNEY BEAN SALAD

Serves 6

3 c. cooked kidney beans	2 onions, chopped(or chives)
1/3 c. mayonnaise	½ cucumber, sliced
½ tsp. strong mustard	¾ c. celery chopped
½ tsp. ea. salt and pepper	4 hard boiled eggs

Mix all ingredients except for kidney beans and hard boiled eggs with mayonnaise. Then when mixed well, add beans and eggs. Mix gently. Cover and chill overnight.

Variation: Instead of mayonnaise, add kidney beans to the following mixture:

½ c. oil	½ -1 clove garlic, crushed
3 Tbs. chopped chives	3 Tbs. chopped parsley
½ c. wine vinegar	capers, basil, tarragon, cayenne, Tabasco and salt to taste

Chill at least 4 to 5 hours.

KENSCOFF SALAD

sweet potatoes, cooked, peeled, sliced	quartered hard-boiled eggs
cucumbers, cut into quarters, seeded, salted and allowed to drain	tomatoes, peeled, seeded and sliced
nasturtium blossoms	
mayonnaise	

Arrange all ingredients artistically on a serving platter. Just before serving, pour over them a few tablespoonfuls of vinaigrette sauce (Recipe follows)

VINAIGRETTE:

3 Tbs. oil	salt and pepper to taste
1 Tbs. vinegar	mustard to taste
parsley, chopped	

Avocados Stuffed With Crab Meat

½ lb. crab meat (fresh or canned)	½ tsp. Worcestershire sauce
3 avocados	few drops Tabasco
¾ c. celery, chopped	2 Tbl. chili sauce or Catsup
1 c mayonnaise	¼ tsp. rosemary, crushed

Cut avocados in half, remove seeds and brush with lime juice. Mix shredded crab meat with celery and just enough mayonnaise to bind. Fill the halves. Make a dressing by mixing the remaining mayonnaise and other ingredients. Serve avocados with the dressing, surrounded by lettuce leaves.

Stuffed Avocado Halves
Serves 2

1 large avocado, ripe but firm	¼ tsp. hot pepper sauce
¼ c. mayonnaise	½ tsp. paprika
20 peeled boiled small shrimp	½ tsp. lime (or lemon) juice

Mix the mayonnaise and seasonings together. Fold in the shrimp. Cut the avocado in half. Do not peel avocado halves. Spoon half the shrimp mixture into each avocado half and serve on lettuce.

Hot Avocado Bowls
Heat to boiling

¾ c. salad oil	¼ c. vinegar
⅛ tsp. Tabasco sauce	2 tsp. sugar
½ tsp. salt	

Add

1 Tbs. chopped onions	1 tsp. Worcestershire sauce
1 Tbs. parsley	1 tsp. dry mustard
2 eggs, hard-boiled, grated	

Fill unchilled avocado halves with this hot dressing and serve as a first course.

TOMATO SALAD

Peel desired number of tomatoes. This can be done easily by plunging each tomato in boiling water, then into iced water for a few seconds. Peel tomatoes. If they have a lot of seeds and liquid, press them out. Slice and sprinkle with salt and pinch of sugar (optional). Drain after half an hour and season with vinaigrette, parsley and chopped shallots. Chill.

BEAN SALAD

4 Tbs. olive oil	1 to 2 c. cooked kidney beans
1 large onion, sliced thin	1 hard-boiled egg, chopped
salt and pepper to taste	1 lb. green beans, cut in half, cooked and cooled
Parmesan cheese, grated, (or substitute Swiss)	1 clove garlic, finely chopped or put through garlic press

Place green beans and kidney beans in large bowl. Combine olive oil, onion, garlic, parsley, salt and pepper. Pour over beans and mix lightly, cover and chill in the refrigerator. Serve on lettuce and sprinkle with chopped egg and cheese.

MOUNTAIN SALAD

3 hard-boiled eggs	1 militon
2 large carrots	1 c. peas
2 large potatoes	1 c. string beans
½ c. bean sprouts	2 medium beets
2 Tbs. chopped celery leaves	2 Tbs. chopped parsley
3 Tbs. mayonnaise	1 small turnip
1 Tbs. vinegar	1 small zucchini

Boil and peel militon, carrots, potatoes, beets, turnip and zucchini. Boil peas and string beans. Cut cooked vegetables into ½ inch cubes; cube eggs; add peas and string beans. Mix with parsley, celery leaves, mayonnaise and vinegar. Add salt and pepper to taste.

FRENCH STYLE LETTUCE SALAD

Serves 4-6

1 head lettuce	¼ tsp. salt
1 clove garlic, sliced	black pepper to taste
2 Tbs. salad oil	1 Tbs. minced parsley
1 Tbs. wine vinegar	1 tsp. lime juice

Wash, drain, and thoroughly dry the lettuce. Rub a salad bowl with garlic and add the other ingredients (except lettuce) to the bowl. Mix well with salad spoon. Crisscross salad fork and spoon in salad bowl to keep lettuce from dressing until ready to serve. With hands, tear lettuce leaves and place over top of salad fork and spoon. Just before serving, toss thoroughly.

HOLIDAY VEGETABLE TOSS

SERVES 6

1 c. shell macaroni	¼ c. chopped green onion
1 c. broccoli flowerets	1 tomato, seeded, chopped
½ c. cauliflower flowerets	1/3 c. Italian salad dressing
½ c. sliced mushrooms	1 medium avocado, peeled, sliced
½ c. shredded carrots	½ c. sliced pitted ripe olives
1 c. sunflower seeds	4-6 artichoke hearts cooked
(optional)	and drained

Cook macaroni; drain; rinse with cold water; and drain well again. In a large bowl combine all ingredients except for the avocado, tomato, and sunflower seeds. Toss with Italian dressing. Cover and chill several hours. At serving time, toss vegetable mixture with avocado, tomato and sunflower seeds.

FESTIVE CITRUS SALAD

Serves 8

3 small grapefruit, peeled
3 oranges, peeled
½ tsp. salt
1 medium cucumber, thinly sliced
2 avocados, seeded, peeled, and sliced
lettuce

orange juice
$^2/_3$ c. wine vinegar
$^1/_3$ c. sugar
sunflower seed(or any nuts of your choice)
1 small onion, thinly sliced and separated into rings
¼ tsp. black pepper

Section grapefruit and oranges over a small bowl to catch juice; reserve juice. In a large bowl combine citrus sections, cucumber, onion, and avocado slices. Measure reserved fruit juices; add orange juice to make 1 cup. Combine juice mixture, vinegar, sugar, salt, and black pepper; pour over fruit. Cover and marinate in refrigerator for 2 to 3 hours. At serving time, mix in nuts and stir until coated. Then use a slotted spoon to remove fruit from marinade. Arrange on lettuce-lined plates. Drizzle some of the marinade on top of each salad.

FRUIT SALAD

2 oranges
3 bananas
½ c. melon balls
½ c. strawberries

4 slices pineapple diced
½ c. raspberries
24 roasted nuts

Combine all ingredients. Mix the following ingredients together and pour over the fruit:

¼ c. pineapple juice
¼ c. lime juice
1 c. sweetened condensed milk beaten with 2 eggs.
Top with grated coconut (optional)

HEART OF PALM SALAD

heart of palm
lettuce
stuffed olives
green pepper rings

chopped parsley
paprika
French dressing

Cut the heart of palm into lengthwise strips and place on lettuce. Garnish with olives and green pepper rings. Sprinkle top with parsley and paprika. Pour dressing over salad before serving.

OIL AND VINEGAR SALAD DRESSING

$1/3$ c. red wine vinegar
$1/4$ c. olive oil

$1/4$ c. sugar
$1/4$ tsp. salt (to taste)

Dissolve the sugar and salt in the vinegar. Add the oil and stir well.

Variation: Add a quarter cup of minced onion or shallots and/or a teaspoon of chopped herbs such as parsley, cilantro, basil, chives, or oregano.

ORANGE HONEY SALAD DRESSING

$1/4$ c. honey
1 c. fresh orange juice
$1/8$ c. fresh lemon juice

$1/2$ tsp. vanilla extract
1 tsp. orange zest
$1/2$ tsp. fresh grated ginger

Stir all ingredients together in a glass container and let the mixture stand in the refrigerator for an hour before use. Excellent on salads that contain fruit.

Dijon Vinaigrette Salad Dressing

¼ c. white wine vinegar
¾ c. olive oil

2 tsp. Dijon mustard
½ tsp. salt

Whisk all ingredients together well or mix in blender.

Caesar Salad Dressing

3 fresh eggs
¾ c. olive oil
¼ c. fesh lemon juice
1 c. feshly grated
    parmesean cheese

1 tsp. salt
1 tsp. mustard powder
2 coves garlic minced
4 achovies in oil

Blend all ingredients together in a food processor or blender.

Spicy Ginger Salad Dressing

¼ c. white wine vinegar
½ c. olive oil
¼ c. sesame oil
½ tsp. salt

1 clove fresh garlic minced
1 tsp. soy sauce
1 Tbs. fresh grated ginger
½ - 1 Habanero pepper

Whisk all ingredients together well or mix in blender. Adjust the amount of Habanero pepper to taste. This goes well on sliced avocados and onions topped with chilled shrimp.

*Haitian Proverb: Don't throw away the old pot
for the new!*

(Don't forget your old friends.)

RICE DISHES AND VEGETABLES

EGGPLANT CASSEROLE

2 medium eggplant	1 medium onion, diced
1 can diced tomatoes	3 cloves garlic, minced
¼ c. Parmesan cheese, grated	1 Tbl. tomato paste
2 sprigs fresh thyme	¼ c. breadcrumbs
2 tsp. parsley, chopped	salt and pepper to taste
¼ tsp. oregano	2 Tbl. olive oil

Peel the eggplant and cut into small pieces. Put eggplant in a large pot and cover with water. Add a little salt and boil until the eggplant is cooked (about 20 - 30 minutes). While the eggplant is cooking, heat the oil in a skillet and lightly brown the onion. Add the garlic and other spices when the onion is almost done.

Place the onion mixture in a bowl. Drain the tomatoes and add to the onions. Drain the cooked eggplant and add to the onions and tomatoes. Mash this mixture with a potato masher or a fork. Using a blender will make the ingredients separate and turn watery. Stir in the Parmesan cheese. Put the mixture into an ovenproof casserole dish and sprinkle with the bread crumbs. Bake in a 350 degree oven until bubbly, about 10 – 15 minutes.

NOTE: The mixture can be prepared in advance and refrigerated, adding the bread crumbs at the time of baking.

PIPERONATA

3 c. sliced onions	1 Tbs. red wine vinegar
¼ tsp. black pepper	¾ tsp. salt
¼ c. oil	4 or 5 large tomatoes,
large green peppers cut	(or canned tomatoes,
into ½" strips	drained)

Sauté onions in oil until soft and lightly browned. Add pepper strips. Cook covered for 10 minutes, stirring frequently.

Add other ingredients, cover and continue cooking until peppers are tender (5 to 10 minutes).

Remove cover. Stir over high heat until liquid has evaporated. The mixture should be thick.

BAKED EGGPLANT

Marinate slices of eggplant about 15 minutes in French dressing. Bake in hot oven about 15 minutes. Turn over. Bake another 5 minutes. Just before serving, add lemon juice and sprinkle with chopped parsley.

EGGPLANT PARMESAN

Serves 6

1 medium eggplant	2 green peppers, chopped
1 c. bread crumbs	2 onions, chopped
½ c. Parmesan cheese	¼ tsp. thyme
2 Tbs. chopped parsley	2 Tbs. oil
1 tsp. salt	1 tsp. oregano
$\frac{1}{8}$ tsp. black pepper	3 Tbs. tomato paste
1 clove garlic, minced	1 to 2 c. grated Swiss cheese
4 tomatoes, chopped	¼ c. additional Parmesan

Preheat oven to 375 degrees.

Cut eggplant into ½ inch slices. Cover eggplant completely with hot water and let stand 5 minutes. Dry slices. Fry in $\frac{1}{3}$ c. oil until lightly browned. Sprinkle with salt and pepper. Put in bottom of 9" x 13" baking pan. Combine next seven ingredients in a blender and blend well. Sprinkle mixture over the eggplant.

In a saucepan, combine tomatoes, green peppers, onions, oil, garlic, and tomato paste and let simmer uncovered about 20 minutes. Spread on top of crumb mixture and eggplant. Top with Swiss cheese and the rest of the Parmesan cheese. Bake 10-15 minutes. Can be made ahead, refrigerated, and baked when ready to use.

STUFFED WHOLE CABBAGE

Remove large outer leaves from one large head of cabbage and set aside. Plunge both the cabbage and the reserved leaves into salted boiling water. After 15 minutes, remove, rinse thoroughly in cold water. Set the cabbage, stem side down, on a square of cheese-cloth. Part the leaves carefully and remove the heart. Reserve the heart for stuffing. Replace the heart with a ball of the stuffing recipe below and continue inserting stuffing between leaves. When the cabbage is full, brush it well with oil and tie the four corners of the cheese-cloth together into a bundle. Set this bundle in a well-greased baking dish. (Instead of brushing with oil, slices of butter or bacon can be laid over the cabbage.) Pour bouillon around cabbage. Cover the dish and bake in fairly hot oven (375 degrees) about an hour. Remove cover and continue basting until cabbage is thoroughly cooked. The sauce should have reduced considerably. Remove cheese-cloth. Serve cabbage and sauce.

Stuffing:

For a large cabbage:

1 lb. ground meat	¼ c. milk
1 medium onion, chopped	2 tsp. salt
¼ c. rice, cooked	$1/_8$ tsp. black pepper

Combine all ingredients with the chopped heart of cabbage and outer leaves.

Haitian Proverb: Telling all is not a joke.

(Telling secrets has consequences.)

Haitian Proverb: Telling is a jewel.

(Everyone likes to be the one to tell something.)

STUFFED CABBAGE LEAVES

Soften the leaves (10 for 1 lb. of meat) a few minutes in very little water over low heat. Fill leaves with stuffing. Use the stuffing recipe in Stuffed Cabbage (See Index), only omitting leaves and heart. Fold back two sides, then roll each leaf. Secure with toothpicks. Arrange in Pyrex or other oven dish.

Baste with: 1) 1 can concentrated tomato sauce

      or 2) well seasoned brown gravy.

Cover the dish. Bake in hot oven (400 degrees) one hour, then reduce heat to 325 degrees and cook ½ hour more.

CABBAGE CASSEROLE

3 lb. cabbage, chopped or shredded
1 lb. onions, sliced
½ c. butter or butter
2½ c. crushed cheese crackers, reserve ½ c.

1 can condensed cream of mushroom soup
4 Tbs. flour
2 c. milk
4 Tbs. butter

Preheat oven to 375 degrees. Cook cabbage in boiling water for 7 minutes. Cook onion slices in boiling salted water until tender. Place layer of cabbage in 2-quart casserole, a layer of onions, and layer of cheese cracker crumbs. Dot with ½ c. butter. Make sauce of remaining butter, flour, salt, and milk. Combine with mushroom soup and pour over top. Sprinkle with ½ c. reserved cracker crumbs. Bake 30 minutes.

PUREED BREADFRUIT NUTS

Remove brown skin (before or after partial cooking).

Put into cold salted water and boil until tender. Remove second skin, and puree the seeds. Return them to a pan of water over low heat.

Add: 1 tablespoon butter

½ c. cream or evaporated milk

Season to taste with salt, pepper and nutmeg.

MILITON / CHAYOTE

A 1 lb. militon takes about an hour to cook in boiling salted water; serve whole, diced, coarsely grated or even cut into match sticks.

MILITON / CHAYOTE WITH BÉCHAMEL SAUCE

Pour Béchamel sauce (See Index) over cooked militon with bread crumbs; heat in oven.

MILITON / CHAYOTE CROQUETTES

| 3 militon | 1 c. bread crumbs |
| 3 eggs | salt and pepper |

Cook militon in their skins. Peel the cooked militon and let dry to eliminate a maximum of liquid.

Put the militon through a food mill, press in cheese cloth or nylon hose to extract more liquid. Mix pulp with 2 eggs and shape into croquettes, adding flour if necessary. Beat third egg with small quantity of water. Dip croquettes in bread crumbs, then in beaten egg, then again in bread crumbs. Deep-fry or pan-fry.

CURRIED MILITON / CHAYOTE

Cook militon in boiling salted water, slice, dice or cut into sticks. Sauté some chopped onions in butter with 1 Tbs. curry powder (more or less, to taste), add in militon and heat thoroughly, mixing well.

CHEESY MILITON / CHAYOTE CASSEROLE

3 militon, boiled	salt and pepper
1 c. grated cheese	minced parsley
¼ c. milk or water	1 Tbs. butter

Mash pulp of cooked militon and mix with other ingredients. Pour into buttered casserole and brown in oven. (About 40 minutes)

Variation: Add 1 clove of crushed garlic to mixture before baking.

CORN FRITTERS

1 10 oz can corn, drained	pinch of salt
½ c. flour	1 c. water
¼ c. butter	3 eggs

Mix flour, butter, salt, water, and 3 eggs. Pour corn into batter and mix well. Drop by tablespoons into very hot oil. Brown and drain on paper towel. Serve with tomato sauce.

Haitian Proverb: The mouth eats every kind of food, but the mouth doesn't speak every kind of word.

(The mouth eats anything but must say everything.)

POLENTA / CORN MEAL MUSH

1 c. corn meal	1 Habanero pepper
3-4 c. water	parsley
salt and pepper	1 Tbs. oil

Mix corn meal with one cup water and add slowly to rest of water when it boils, with oil and seasoning. Cook over low heat, stirring frequently. After 5 minutes of cooking insert the Habanero pepper whole. Keep stirring until cooked. Be careful not to break the pepper. Being whole it will impart a wonderful aroma but not too much heat.

Variations: When water boils, add corn meal, stirring constantly. Lightly fry spices in butter or oil, and add to corn meal. Remove from heat and add butter before serving.

One or two cups chopped meat or ham, fried with garlic and onion in oil, or plain, can be added into the water with the corn meal.

1 cup grated coconut is another tasty addition.

RED POLENTA

(Corn Meal Mush with Kidney Beans)

Cook beans until they are tender, or about to burst. Drain, reserving the liquid. Gently fry beans in butter or fat with crushed garlic, parsley and Habanero pepper. Add in the bean liquid plus the quantity of water required to cook the corn meal. Season to taste, add corn meal mixed with cold water (1 c. corn meal per 3-4 c. water) and stir frequently until meal is cooked. Before serving, add butter.

CREOLE POLENTA

4 c. hot cooked corn meal mush	pinch "malaguette" of oregano or marjoram
¼ c. chopped onion	6 cloves
1 c. chopped green pepper	¼ c. grated cheese
2 c. chopped tomatoes	½ c. milk (optional)
1 Tbs. salt	½ c. chopped parsley
3 Tbs. oil	

Gently fry onion and pepper in oil. Add tomatoes and spices and simmer 10 minutes. Pour cooked mush into this mixture. Stir and pour in buttered pan or oven dish. Sprinkle with cheese. Bake about 20 minutes in hot oven. (450 degrees)

SEASONED POTATOES

10 small potatoes	2 Tbl. parsley, chopped fine
3 Tbs. olive oil	½ tsp. coarse salt
2 cloves garlic, crushed	black pepper to taste

Preheat oven to 400 degrees. Using small new potatoes or Russet variety, wash potatoes but do not peel. Potatoes should be about the size of a golf ball. If larger, cut into two pieces. Mix other ingredients together and rub the potatoes, completely coating them, with the mixture. Put the potatoes on a rack that has been placed on a cookie sheet. Bake in oven until done, approximately 30 – 40 minutes.

GRILLED VEGETABLES

Serves 6

2 medium zucchini	3 cloves garlic, minced
2 medium yellow squash	½ tsp. coarse salt
1 bulb of fennel	3 Tbl. olive oil
8 oz. whole mushrooms	1 tsp. fresh thyme
2 medium onions	1 tsp. parsley, chopped fine
6 - 8 fingerling potatoes	2 tsp. crushed rosemary
2 small parsnips	¼ tsp. black pepper

Preheat oven to 400 degrees. Wash vegetables. Cut zucchini, yellow squash and parsnips into one inch pieces. Separate fennel bulb into strips. Cut each onion into quarters and gently separate pieces. Leave fingerling potatoes whole.

Mix the oil and spices (except the salt) together. Place in large bowl. Add vegetables and toss until each piece is generously coated.

Arrange the vegetables on a cookie sheet. Try to leave a little space around each piece. (Use two cookie sheets if necessary.) Place in hot oven and bake for 20 minutes. Reduce heat to 325 degrees and continue baking for 20 minutes. Sprinkle with coarse salt and bake 5 more minutes. Remove and serve hot.

Variation: Try adding or substituting your favorite vegetables in the above. Suggestions include sweet potatoes, turnips, carrots, cauliflower, celery, plantain, and yams.

Haitian Proverb: Walk slowly, and carry good news.

(Take your time and bring back good news.
Get the job done right.)

VEGETABLE SAUTÉ

Serves 2

3 c. torn fresh spinach	1 c. red cabbage, in 1" pieces
½ tsp. instant chicken bouillon granules	½ c. coarsely shredded carrot (1 medium)
¼ tsp. dried basil, crushed	½ tsp. sugar

In an 8 inch skillet cook spinach in a small amount of boiling water just until wilted. Remove to serving plate. In same skillet combine the 3 Tbs. water, bouillon granules, sugar, and basil. Bring mixture to boiling. Add cabbage and carrot. Reduce heat; cover and simmer 3 minutes. Serve at once on top of the spinach.

STEAMED ZUCCHINI AND CARROTS

Serves 4

2 large zucchini, sliced in medium strips	4 large carrots, sliced in medium strips
1 green pepper, chopped	1 onion chopped
2 Tbs. butter	2 tsp. lime juice
1 clove garlic	paprika
1 tsp. celery salt	

Steam carrots until almost tender; then put in zucchini and finish cooking until both carrots and zucchini are tender but not mushy.

Meanwhile, while the vegetables are cooking, sauté green pepper and onion in the butter and garlic. Add lime juice and seasonings. Keep warm until vegetables are done. Remove garlic clove. Pour over vegetables and serve. Sprinkle with slivered almonds, if desired.

GARLIC AND ONIONS CARROTS

3 medium carrots, crinkle cut	2 tsp. butter
½ c. small whole onions	1 clove garlic, minced
salt and pepper	1 tsp. lime juice

Cook carrots for 5-6 minutes. Combine onions, butter, garlic, lime, salt and pepper. Cook and stir 3 minutes. Add carrots, cook two more minutes.

Tom Tom (Mashed Breadfruit with Okra)

Serves 4

1 breadfruit	½ tsp. salt
1 cup crab meat or 4 crabs	¼ tsp. black pepper
2 cups sliced okra	¼ tsp. fresh thyme
¼ c. onion, chopped	2 cloves garlic, minced
1 Tbs. parsley, minced	1 Habanero pepper
1Tbs. olive oil	

Boil the breadfruit and then peel it, remove the core and purée it in a food processor.

Cut the okra into ½ inch slices and boil it with the crab meat or crabs and the rest of the seasoning ingredients in 3 cups of water. Simmer gently stirring frequently until the okra is tender and most of the water has evaporated.

Serve over the pureed breadfruit.

Variation: Use plantain instead of breadfruit.

MASHED BREADFRUIT

1 ripe breadfruit	salt and pepper to taste
¼ c milk or cream	1 Tbl. butter

Cut the breadfruit into quarters and boil covered with water until tender. Remove and peel. Put the pulp in a mixer and beat, gradually adding the cream or milk. When the consistency is that of mashed potatoes add the seasonings and butter. Serve warm.

BAKED BREADFRUIT

Poke holes in a mature, but not too ripe breadfruit. Bake whole until soft. Quarter and serve hot with butter and salt and pepper.

NOTE: Be sure to poke holes before baking, otherwise the breadfruit might "explode" in the oven.

CORN PUDDING

1 Tbs. cornstarch	2 eggs, beaten well
1 Tbs. flour	½ c. milk
1 Tbs. sugar	1 tsp. vanilla
1 can creamed corn	3 Tbs. butter, melted
salt to taste	

Combine in a saucepan cornstarch, flour, sugar, and salt. Stir in corn and beaten eggs. Add milk, vanilla and butter. Mix well and pour into a shallow casserole. Bake for about one hour.

Haitian proverb: After harvesting the corn, we'll count the sprouts.

(Don't count on results prematurely.)

STEWED GREEN PAPAYA

Peel and slice one very green, medium sized papaya. There should be about two cups of fruit. Drop it into rapidly boiling salted water. Simmer for about one-half hour, or until fruit is tender. Drain well. An excellent side dish to stews.

Add:

> 1 Tbs. butter
> Dash of nutmeg

HOT POTATO AND BROCCOLI SALAD

Serves 3

1 lb. tiny new potatoes	½ tsp. dry mustard
1 lb. broccoli flowerets	¼ tsp. paprika
⅓ c. olive oil	salt and pepper to taste
1 clove garlic, finely minced or pressed	2 `green onions finely sliced
5 Tbs. cider vinegar	

Cook potatoes whole in their jackets until just tender, about 20 minutes. Drain, do not peel, cube; keep warm.

Steam broccoli until just tender, cut into small pieces and keep warm.

While vegetables are cooking combine remaining ingredients in small pot and bring to a boil; stir. Arrange vegetables in serving dish; pour on vinaigrette; toss and serve.

GRILLED EGGPLANT PUREE

Serves 4

2 medium eggplant	1 clove garlic, crushed
2 tsp. olive oil	salt and pepper to taste
1 small onion, chopped	¼ c parmesan cheese, grated

Wash and dry eggplant. Leaving whole, poke each eggplant with a few holes. Place on grill and cook until tender. Cut each eggplant in two and scoop out the cooked pulp. (This part can be done in advance and pulp can be refrigerated until needed.)

Sauté onion in the olive oil until translucent. Add garlic and stir for two mintues. Remove from heat. Combine onion mixture and eggplant pulp in a blender and mix until pureed. Add salt and pepper to taste. Place in oven proof dish and sprinkle with parmesan cheese. Bake until hot and golden.

SWEET-SOUR CUCUMBERS

½ c. white vinegar	¼ tsp. white pepper
⅓ c. salad oil	¼ tsp. oregano leaves
2 Tbs. sugar	3 medium cucumbers, thinly sliced
¾ tsp. salt	

In large bowl, combine all ingredients. Cover and refrigerate at least 45 minutes to blend flavors, stirring occasionally.

Haitian Proverb: "God is not Father-in Law, He is Father."

RICE WITH BLACK MUSHROOMS (DIRI DJON DJON)

Serves 6

1 c. dried Haitian djon djon mushrooms without stems or dried black European mushrooms

¼ c. finely chopped green pepper

1 Tbs. vegetable oil

1 oz. salt pork, cut into ¼ inch diced cubes

2 c. boiling water

1 tsp. salt

1 Tbs. finely chopped scallions, including one inch of the green tops

¼ c. finely chopped fresh parsley

1 tsp. finely chopped garlic

2 c. uncooked long-grain white rice

¼ tsp. dried thyme, crumbed

pinch of ground cloves

Place mushrooms in a small enameled, stainless steel or glass saucepan and pour in 3 c. of boiling water. Let the mushrooms soak for 30 minutes, then bring them to a boil over high heat. Reduce the heat to low and simmer uncovered for 15 minutes. Drain the mushrooms, reserving the liquid.

In a heavy 3 to 4 quart saucepan, heat the oil over moderate heat until a light haze forms above it. Fry the pork in the oil, turning until crisp and brown. With a slotted spoon, transfer the pork to paper towels to drain. Add green pepper, parsley, scallions and garlic to the fat remaining in the pan and stir for about two minutes, until the vegetables are soft but not brown.

Add the rice and stir constantly for 2 or 3 minutes, until the grains turn somewhat milky and opaque. Do not let them brown. Combine the reserved mushroom cooking liquid with enough boiling water to make four cups and pour the mixture over the rice. Stir the mushrooms, pork, thyme, cloves and salt, and bring to a boil over high heat. Reduce the heat to low, cover tightly, and simmer for about 20 - 30 minutes or until the rice has absorbed all the liquid in the pan and becomes a rich walnut brown color. Taste for seasonings, fluff the rice with a fork, and serve.

RICE AND BEANS (DIRI AK PWA / DIRI KOLE)

This is considered Haiti's National Dish

Serves 6

1 c. dried red kidney beans	3 cloves minced garlic
1½ tsp. salt	3 Tbs. butter or oil
½ tsp. black pepper	6-8 c. water
12 whole cloves	2 c. uncooked long-grain white rice
1 tsp. fresh thyme	chicken stock - optional

In a large sieve or colander wash the beans under running water. Transfer to a heavy 3-4 quart saucepan; add half the salt and spices plus 6 c. of water. Bring to a boil over high heat; reduce to low, and simmer partially covered for 1-2 hours until the beans are tender but still whole. Drain in a sieve, reserving the bean liquid.

Melt the butter or oil in a heavy skillet, drop in the beans and stir for 1 minute. Add the rice and stir for 1-2 minutes more until the rice grains turn somewhat milky and opaque. Add the remaining cloves, thyme and garlic and stir for 30 seconds.

Add the reserved liquid the beans were cooked in plus enough water or chicken stock to make 4 cups. Boil about 5 minutes or until some of the liquid begins to be absorbed by the rice. Cover and reduce the heat to low. Simmer for 30-40 minutes until the rice is tender and has absorbed all of the liquid. Taste for seasonings and set off the heat, partially covered to keep hot.

Fluff the rice and beans with a fork and serve hot.

Variations: For added flavor put a whole Habanero pepper on top of the rice and beans when you cover the pot and reduce the heat to low. Because the pepper is not cut it will add more flavor than heat to the dish.

PIGEON PEAS AND RICE

Serves 4

1 c. dried pigeon peas	sprig fresh, thyme
4 c. fresh water	2 Tbs. butter
2 cloves garlic, minced	1 c. rice
1 medium onion, minced	salt and pepper

Soak pigeon peas overnight in water. Drain them well and place peas in a heavy kettle. Add water, garlic, onion, thyme, butter, salt and pepper. Bring to a boil, reduce heat and simmer for about one-half hour. Add this to rice. (If fresh peas are used, add one-half pound of peas to the kettle when you add the rice). There should be about two and one-half cups of liquid with the peas and rice. Simmer the combined ingredients for 20 – 30 minutes, until rice is fluffy and the water is absorbed. This dish may be served either hot or cold.

RICE AND CHEESE STUFFING

2 c. cooked rice	½ tsp. salt
½ c. milk	2 Tbs. melted butter
2 Tbs. pimento, chopped fine	1 Tbs. parsley
1 c. American or Swiss cheese, diced	black pepper and paprika to taste
1 Tbs. onion, grated	

Mix all ingredients well and use to stuff peppers or tomatoes.

Bake about 30 - 40 minutes in moderate oven.

RICE AND VEGETABLES
Serves 4

1 ½ c. rice	1 Tbs. olive oil
1 c. cooked peas	1 Tbl. shallot, chopped
2 cloves garlic, minced	1 tsp. chopped parsley
½ c. shredded carrots	sprig fresh, thyme
4 c. water	salt and pepper to taste

Heat the olive oil in a sauce pan large enough to cook the rice. Add the garlic, thyme, shallot and carrots. Stir for about one minute and then add the water and peas. Bring to a boil. Add rice and cook at low boil uncovered until the liquid cooks down to just above rice. Reduce heat, cover and cook until rice is done, about 20 minutes more.

CREOLE STUFFED TOMATOES
Serves 4

2 c. cooked white rice	½ tsp. cayenne pepper
4 large firm tomatoes	1 tsp. thyme
1 Tbl. olive oil	½ tsp. cumin
1 tsp. paprika	½ c. chopped green pepper

Core the tomatoes, being careful to leave whole. Place in ovenproof dish. Heat the olive oil in a sauce pan and stir in green peppers. When peppers are tender remove from heat. Add spices and rice and toss until well mixed. Stuff each tomato with ½ cup of rice mixture. Bake in 350 degree oven until heated throughout.

Variation: Add ½ cup spicy sausage pieces to rice.

CURRIED RICE

Serves 4

4 c. hot water	½ c. sliced green peppers
1 c. rice	4 Tbs. melted butter
1 c. tomatoes	1½ tsp. curry powder
½ c. finely sliced onions	

Pour hot water over rice and place it where it will remain hot, but will not cook, for about 45 minutes. Preheat oven to 350 degrees.

Add to the rice the rest of the ingredients and bake in a baking dish for 1½ hours or until done. Stir occasionally. Remove dish from oven while the rice is still moist.

FRIED RICE I

Serves 4

2 eggs slightly beaten	2 Tbs. soy sauce
½ c. frozen peas, thawed	3 c. cooked rice
1 tsp. salt	2 green onions, chopped
½ c. canned mushrooms diced	1 c. chicken, shrimp(any leftover meat diced)
5 Tbs. oil for frying	

Prepare vegetables. Heat 1 Tbs. oil in frying pan until hot. Add eggs and stir until soft-scrambled. Remove from pan. Add 2 Tbs. oil, peas, salt and mushrooms and stir-fry for 1 minute. Remove from pan. Remove pan from burner wipe with paper towel. Return to burner and add remaining oil and heat. Add rice and stir until hot. Add soy sauce and continue stirring until well mixed. Add green onions, meat, and return remaining ingredients to pan and stir-fry for 1 – 2 minutes.

FRIED RICE II

Serves 4

2 c. cooked , cold white rice
½ c. soy sauce.
1 c. beans sprouts, fresh or canned
½ c. mushrooms, water chestnuts or bamboo shoots

½ c. carrots, shredded
½-1 c. cooking oil
2 c. Chinese cabbage, shredded
2 c. thinly sliced uncooked chicken, rabbit, pork or beef (marinated in ½ c. soy sauce)

It is easier to slice the meat into thin slices it it is partially frozen.

Heat 2 Tbs. oil in wok or large skillet. Add cabbage and stir fry until limp and tender. Remove, leaving as much oil as possible. Place cabbage in large bowl and keep warm. Repeat this process with all the vegetables, adding oil only when necessary. Cook the meat in the same way. Drain and save the meat juices and soy sauce. Add the meat to the vegetables.

In ¼ c. hot oil, stir fry the rice, stirring constantly to avoid sticking. The rice may have to be cooked in 2 or 3 batches. While stirring the rice add the saved soy sauce and meat juices.   Add the vegetables and meat to the rice. Mix well and serve hot.

WHITE RICE

Serves 4

2 c. rice
½ tsp. salt

1 tsp. oil
5 c. water

Heat water to boiling, add salt and oil. Clean and rinse rice 3 times, changing water each time. Add the rice to boiling water. Simmer uncovered 20 - 30 minutes or until water level is almost equal with rice. Reduce heat and cover 15 - 20 minutes longer or until all liquid is absorbed.

Variation: Sauté 1 crushed clove of garlic or 1 chopped onion in oil. Add water and continue as above.

May be served with Red Bean Sauce. (See Index)

TWICE COOKED PLANTAIN (BANNANN PEZE)

Vegetable oil   2 large green plantain
                                 Salt

Peel plantain skin as shown (See Index). With your fingers pull the skin away from the white banana-like fruit inside and pull or cut off the fibrous strings. Slice the plantain crosswise into ½ inch pieces.

In a heavy 12 inch skillet, heat the oil over moderate heat until a light haze forms above it. Add as many plantain slices as you can without crowding the pan, and brown for about 2 minutes on each side. As they crown, transfer them to paper towels to drain. On a board, using a broad solid (not slotted) spatula, press each slice into a flat round about ¼ inch thick and 2 inches in diameter. Reheat the oil and fry the rounds again for about 1 minute on each side or until golden. Drain on paper towels and sprinkle with salt. Serve warm with Pikliz Relish (See Index).

NOTE: The plantain can be prepared ahead and saved after being pressed and the second frying done right before serving.

BOILED CORN ON THE COB (MAYI BOUYI)

Mature corn: Boil cobs of dry corn without husks in heavily salted water until the kernels swell and begin to get tender. Remove the cobs of corn from the water and make knife cut marks about a quarter of the way into the kernels. This will allow the salt flavor to penetrate into the corn. Return the cobs to the water and continue boiling until tender.

Variation: Add one or two Habanero peppers to the water when boiling.

Sweet corn: Bring a pot of water to a boil. Add cobs of fresh corn and boil for 15 minutes. Remove from the water cover with melted butter and sprinkle with salt.

ROASTED CORN ON THE COB (MAYI BOUKANNEN)

Dry corn: Roast cobs of dry corn without husks slowly over fire turning frequently to avoid burning. Corn is done when it becomes golden brown and kernels begin to pop. Serve with lime juice and salt.

Fresh corn: Roast cobs of fresh corn in the husk slowly over fire turning frequently to avoid burning. Corn is done when it becomes golden. Serve with butter and salt.

ONION TART

Serves 6-8

6 c. coarsely diced onions	1 c. Parmesan cheese, shredded
¼ c. flour	½ c. milk
¼ c. butter	¼ c. shredded country ham

Dissolve the flour in the milk and let stand.

Sauté the onions gently in the butter until they become translucent. Stir in the shredded ham. Pour the milk and flour mixture evenly over the onions. And the cheese and stir gently. Remove from the stove before the cheese sticks to the pan and spred the mixture evenly in a 10 inch lightly greased tart pan.

Bake at 375 degrees for 20 minutes. The tart will become golden and will form a light crust on the bottom which hardens as it cools. Serve warm or cold.

Variations: Bake in a pie crust in the tart pan at 350 degrees for 30 - 40 minutes. City ham or canned ham may be used instead of country ham with the addition of half a teaspoon of salt to the milk and flour.

Oeufs Farcis Au Foie De Poulet

ROYAL HAITIAN HOTEL

(Eggs Stuffed with Chicken Liver Pate)

5 eggs, hard boiled	½ tsp. salt
¼ lb. chicken liver	¼ tsp. onion, chopped
4 slices bacon	1½ to 2 tsp. mayonnaise
¼ Tbs. black pepper	2 green limes
1 Tbs. finely chopped parsley	$1/_8$ Diced Habanero pepper

1½ tsp. chopped chives

Clean liver with cold water and limes. Put liver in pan and pour hot water over to cover. Let cook for 15 to 20 minutes or until tender. Drain and set aside. Next, sauté bacon slices in a saucepan.

Grind liver up. Cut eggs in half lengthwise. Mash egg yolks and mix with pureed liver, ½ Tbs. parsley, pepper, bacon, Habanero pepper, and mayonnaise. Correct seasonings. Fill each egg half with liver mixture. Sprinkle with remaining chopped parsley to decorate.

Haitian Proverb: All lightning bugs shine
for their own eyes.

(Everyone always likes what he or she does.)

Bombay Soup (Creamy Curry and Lobster soup)
LA LANTERNE
Serves 6

fish bones from 2 large
fish (red snapper)
2 pints water
1 small papaya, diced
7 small potatoes, diced

Caribbean lobster - 2-3
pieces per person
soy sauce to taste
salt, white pepper
1 laurel leaf
3 tsp. curry

Boil the fish bones (careful not to use very small bones), lobster, and water together. Boil liquid down to 1 pint. Discard bones and remove lobster and set aside. Add potatoes, papaya, and laurel leaf to the liquid; cook for 5 to 10 minutes. Then put soup in blender and puree. Add salt, white pepper, soy sauce, curry, and lobster; simmer for 10 minutes.

WEST INDIAN PUMPKIN SOUP
VILLA CREOLE
Serves 6-8

1 lb. beef, cubed
3 lb. pumpkin
2 leeks, white & greens diced
2 carrots, diced
1 onion
1 clove garlic
1 bouquet garni

1 bunch celery leaves, minced
3 liters water
¼ lb. spaghetti
juice 1 lime
salt to taste
black pepper to taste
1 Tbs. butter

Cook the meat in 3 liters of water. Add the green parts of the leeks, the onion and garlic. Boil for 1 hour. Put peeled, cleaned, and quartered pumpkin in a separate pan and cook it with water, until tender. Purée the pumpkin, add the bouillon (broth from the meat) and pass it through a sieve.

Return the puree to the pan and simmer with the spaghetti, the diced carrots and leeks, bouquet garni, salt, pepper and celery leaves for 20 to 30 minutes. Before serving, add the lime and butter.

AUBERGINE ET CIRIQUES (EGGPLANT WITH SMALL CRABS)

VILLA CREOLE

1 Tbs. oil	3 lemons or limes
6 small crabs	bouquet garni
1 lb. fresh tomatoes	2 cloves garlic, crushed
1 Habanero pepper	salt and pepper to taste
1 Tbs. butter	4 eggplants
1 onion, diced	

Clean the crabs by rubbing them with a cut lemon. Rinse in cold water. Peel the eggplants and slice them thickly. Boil in water until cooked. In a big saucepan; put the crabs, cut up tomatoes, garlic, onion, Habanero pepper, and oil. Cook covered until most of the liquid has evaporated and the mixture starts to color a little bit. Mash the eggplants with a spoon. Add the butter and lime juice, salt and pepper to taste, crab mixture, and stir thoroughly. Serve warm.

SPRING CHICKENA LA BRUNO

LA LANTERNE

Serves 6

6 young chicken breasts	6 Tbs. each oil & butter
flour	salt and pepper to taste
3 eggs	mustard, Dijon variety
	1 coconut, grated, juice extracted, and dried

Season chicken breasts with salt, pepper, and mustard. Dip chicken in flour; then dip in eggs; and then roll the breasts in the dried coconut.

Put oil and butter in pan and heat until very hot. When you put the chicken in oil, turn heat down. Cook for 10 minutes. Keep turning pieces of chicken. (Watch closely so as not to allow coconut to burn). Serve with French fries and vegetables.

FRENCH PEPPER STEAK

LE TIFFANY

Serves 6

3 lb. filet of beef
2 to 3 Tbs. black pepper
2 Tbs. butter
1 Tbs. mustard

½ c. beef gravy
½ c. fresh cream
1 can onion soup

Rub filet with ½ of the pepper (freshly ground is best) and butter; put under broiler and broil until desired doneness. (Or put on grill)

Mix the rest of the ingredients in saucepan and heat well. If sauce is too runny, add 1 tsp. cornstarch and heat until thick.

When meat is finished cooking, pour sauce on top of filet and serve with French fries, salad, and bread.

TASSOT CREOLE

LE TIFFANY

Serves 6

2 lb. beef, in bite size pieces
1 onion, chopped
1 tomato, chopped
Sprig of parsley

1 diced Habanero pepper
1 clove of garlic, crushed
Salt to taste

Marinate beef with other ingredients for about 4 hours.

Sauté mixture in saucepan until it has color. Remove meat from sauce and put on cookie sheet; place in oven (300 degrees) and bake until crisp. Pour sauce over meat and serve with French fries and salad.

TOURTE AU POULET (CHICKEN PIE)

ROYAL HAITIAN HOTEL

1 c. mixed vegetables,
(carrots, peas, etc.)
¼ lb. butter
¼- ½ c. cold water

1 recipe Easy Chicken
Creole (See Index)
2 c. flour

Sift flour. Work butter into flour with a pastry blender until crumbly. Pour water a little at a time over mixture; mix until dough forms a ball. Let chill for 1 hour. When chilled, divide dough in half for bottom and top crust of pie. Roll ½ out to fit pie pan.

Cook chicken a la Creole. Remove chicken and thicken sauce with cornstarch. Bone and cut up chicken in small pieces. Mix with cooked vegetables and sauce from the chicken. Pour into pie crust and cover with left over dough if desired. Brush top with 1 egg yolk and 1 Tbs. water. Cook 10 minutes at 450 degrees. Reduce to 350 degrees and cook for 15 minutes more.

Haitian Proverb: To be near is not to have arrived.

(Almost is not good enough.)

GATEAU AUX FRUITS RENVERSE (UPSIDE DOWN FRUIT CAKE)

ROYAL HAITIAN HOTEL

1 c. butter
1½ c. sifted sugar
¼Tbs. lemon rind
4 eggs,
   (separated)
3 c. flour, sifted
   vanilla extract to taste
1 Tbs. baking powder
¼ tsp. salt

1 tsp. vanilla
½ c. butter
1 c. brown sugar
4-5 pineapple slices from
   can (save juice)
1 box pitted prunes
   Maraschino cherries
1 c. milk
   (or use ½ c. light cream
   and ½ c. pineapple
   juice)

Line the bottom of greased, 9" x 11" pan first with ½ c. butter; then 1 c. brown sugar; then pineapple slices; then prunes; and then Maraschino cherries. Pour a little pineapple juice over mixture, just enough to dampen sugar.

Mix dry ingredients together and sift. Cream in another bowl one cup butter and 1½ cups sugar. Add 1 egg yolk at a time, beating well after each one. Alternately, in small amounts, add dry ingredients then milk into butter mixture; starting and finishing with dry ingredients. For the last time that you add the milk, add vanilla in with it. Beat egg whites until they form peaks, and add gradually to the batter. Pour dough into pan. Cook for 40 to 45 minutes. Let stand for a few minutes. Turn pan over and remove cake so the pineapple mixture is on top of the cake.

GLAZED AND BRAISED PORK (GRIYO)

Serves 4

¼ c. vegetable oil
2 lb. boneless pork,
    preferably pork loin, cut
    into 2" cubes
1 c. finely chopped onions
¼ c. strained fresh lime juice
½ tsp. fresh thyme
½ tsp. black pepper

1 c. strained orange juice
¼ c. finely chopped shallots
    or ¼ c. finely chopped
    scallions white part only
¼ c. water
¼ tsp. crumbled dried thyme
½ tsp. salt
½ Habanero pepper

Combine all ingredients except the oil and place in refrigerator for 4 - 24 hours. Drain the pork pieces, but save the marinade. In a heavy 12-inch skillet, heat the ¼ cup of vegetable oil over moderate heat until a light haze forms above it. Add the pork cubes. Turn them frequently with a spoon and regulate the heat so that they brown richly and evenly without burning. When all the pork has been browned, add the reserved marinade. Bring to a boil over high heat, cover the pan, lower the heat and simmer for 30 minutes. Then uncover the pan, raise the heat to high and, stirring frequently to prevent the meat from sticking, cook briskly for about 10 minutes, until the sauce thickens to a syrupy glaze.

Serve with Pikliz or Sauce Ti Malice (See Index).

Haitian Proverb: With many hands the load is not heavy.

(Many hands make work light.)

PINEAPPLE PORK CHOPS

Serves 6

6 thick pork chops	6 slices pineapple
2 Tbs. salad oil	½ c. pineapple juice
3 sweet potatoes	lemon juice

Sauté chops on both sides in oil. Sprinkle with salt, peel potatoes and cut in half. Rub with lemon juice. Place on chops, press pineapple on potatoes, add pineapple juice to the chops. Cover, cook on high until steam escapes freely, turn to low. Cook 45 minutes.

GRILLED GOAT

Serves 6

2 legs of goat, cut into 1" pieces, cleaned well	1 c. Bar-B-Q sauce (optional)
2 qt. boiling water	1 Tbs. dark rum
4 Tbs. lemon juice	2 Tbs. butter
2 Tbs. oil	1 Tbs. vinegar
	salt, Habanero pepper, onion, garlic, parsley to taste

Mix water and lemon juice together. Before seasoning the meat, pour the boiling water and lemon juice mixture over the goat. This helps remove the strong smell of the meat. Let it stand for 2 or 3 minutes. Drain and discard the water completely and pour seasoning, vinegar, rum, butter, oil, Bar-B- Q sauce over the meat. Marinade for 3 or more hours.

Put meat and marinade in a saucepan and cook until the meat is tender. (Amount of time depends on piece of meat). Then put the goat on a grill and baste with marinade.

Variation: Substitute lamb in place of goat meat.

CURRIED GOAT

Serves 4-6

¼ c. vegetable oil
2 lb. goat, boneless preferred
2 limes
1 medium onion, chopped
2 c. chicken broth
½ c. coconut milk
2 c. water
1 Tbl. flour

1 small can tomoto paste

3 cloves
3 bay leaves
½ tsp. black pepper
3 cloves garlic, crushed
¼ tsp. ground ginger
1 ½ Tbl. curry powder
salt to taste
1 Habanero pepper
(optional)

Cut goat meat into cubes or small pieces. Wash with juice of limes. Rinse and pat dry. Heat vegetable oil in large pan. Brown goat in oil. Remove and set aside. Sauté onions until translucent. Remove and set aside. Add flour to oil and stir until absorbed (add a little more oil or butter if needed). Gradually add broth, coconut milk and water Stir in tomato paste. Add goat and other ingredients. Bring to a boil. Reduce heat and simmer until cooked, depending on the age of the goat, 40 - 75 minutes.

If the curry sauce is not spicy enough for your tastes, add a little more curry powder or a small piece of Habanero pepper without the seeds. Serve with white or brown rice.

Tip: For the Habanero pepper flavor without all the heat, you can place a whole pepper and simmer with the food being careful not to prick or break the pepper when stirring. Remove pepper before serving food.

Variations: Substitute lamb, pork or beef in place of goat meat.

SLOW ROASTED GOAT

Serves 6

1 leg (shank) of goat (5-6 lb)	6 cloves garlic, peeled
1 lime	¾ c. chicken broth
2 Tbl. olive oil	½ c. white wine
1 Tbl. butter	5 sprigs fresh thyme
4 Tbl. dark rum	salt and pepper to taste

Fill a large stockpot with water and bring to a boil. Rub the goat shank with lime. Put the goat into the boiling water. Return to a boil. Reduce heat and simmer for 15 minutes. Remove goat and pat dry. Season the goat with salt and pepper. Discard water. Heat oven to 250 degrees.

While the oven is heating, melt the butter with the olive oil over medium heat in an oven proof dutch oven. Add the goat and brown on both sides. Pour in the rum and ignite with a match. When the flames subside, add the garlic, thyme, broth and water.

Cover the Dutch oven and place in oven. Cook, turning twice, for 6 - 7 hours, or until the meat is tender. Remove the pan from the oven and transfer the goat to a dish (keeping it warm).

Pour the liquid in the pan through a sieve, pressing on the garlic to extract the cooked flesh. Return the liquid to the pan over high heat and bring to a boil, scraping the pan to loosen any browned bits. Reduce the liquid to a sauce consistency. Taste and adjust salt and pepper, if needed.

Carve the roast and serve with the sauce.

Variation: Substitute lamb in place of goat meat.

RABBIT AND CASHEWS

1 rabbit (deboned & sliced)	1 c. raw cashew nuts (or raw peanuts)
1 medium onion, chopped	¼ c. soy sauce
½ - 1 Habanero pepper	1 Tbs. corn starch
1 can bean sprouts	½ c. cooking oil

Debone the rabbit. This can be done easily by slicing the meat into thin strips while rabbit is partially frozen.

In a wok or large skillet, heat ½ cup oil until very hot. Add the Habanero pepper. Stir fry the onion and bean sprouts until tender. Remove from oil, draining as much as possible and being careful to leave pepper in the oil. Repeat this process with the rabbit, cooking it until it takes on color. Remove the rabbit and discard the pepper entirely. Fry the nuts in the same oil. Drain off any excess oil and return the rabbit, onion, beans sprouts with the nuts to the skillet or wok.

Mix the cornstarch with the soy sauce. Pour over rabbit mixture. Stir and cook until sauce is transparent and heated thoroughly. Serve hot with white rice.

NOTE: This dish is fairly hot. For a milder dish, remove the Habanero pepper sooner or use less of it.

PORK CHOPS WITH VEGETABLES

Brown 2 pork chops in 1 Tbs. melted butter. Add ½ cup sliced carrots, ½ cup sliced green beans, 1 cup diced potatoes, ¼ tsp. basil and 2 envelopes of powdered cream of mushroom soup. Blend with ⅔ cup water. Simmer covered for 45 minutes. Serve with wild rice (may simmer rice with chops).

Chicken With Coconut

2 chickens, about 2½ lb.
each, split into halves.
salt, pepper, flour, oil
2 medium onions, sliced
¾ tsp. curry powder
pinch saffron

3 medium tomatoes,
sliced
⅓ c. grated coconut
3 c. chicken bouillon
1 sliced green pepper
paprika to taste

Put salt, black pepper and flour into a large paper bag. Put chicken in bag and shake until well coated.

Brown chicken in oil in a heavy skillet. Remove from pan, leaving just enough oil to gently cook onions, sliced pepper, tomatoes, curry, saffron and paprika. Return chicken to pan and cook over low heat until tender.

While chicken is cooking, simmer coconut in bouillon 10 minutes. Strain and pour over chicken. Stir well, allow to blend. Serve.

Ratatouille

May be prepared without meat for a vegetarian version.

3 potatoes
3 zucchini
2 onions
4 peeled tomatoes
3 Tbs. lemon juice
½ lb. meat cut in cubes (or
meat balls)

1 large eggplant
3 carrots
2 green peppers
2 Tbs. tomato paste
dash cinnamon

Fry all ingredients in a little oil, 1 or 2 minutes. In a saucepan put 1 layer of vegetables, sprinkle with meat, then another layer of vegetables. Season with salt, pepper and a little bit of cinnamon. Mix tomato sauce with water, lemon juice. Almost cover the vegetables with the sauce and let simmer, until very little liquid is left. Don't stir. Serve with white rice.

Haitian Proverb: "Three women are enough to make a market.
(It doesn't take many women to make a lot of noise.)

CAJUN-STYLE CHICKEN STEW

Serves 6

¼ c. oil	⅛ tsp. hot pepper sauce
¼ c. all purpose flour	1 c. long-grain rice
1 large onion, diced	½ c. okra
1 large celery stalk, diced	½ c. whole-kernel corn
1 medium green pepper, diced	3 c. chopped cooked chicken
1 28-oz can tomatoes	¾ tsp. salt
1 tsp. sugar	

In 12-inch skillet over medium heat, stir flour into hot oil; cook, stirring constantly, until flour is dark brown but not burned. Add onion, celery, and green pepper; cook over medium heat until vegetables are tender, stirring occasionally. Gradually stir in tomatoes with their liquid, sugar, salt, and hot pepper sauce until blended, stirring until boiling. Reduce heat to low; and simmer 10 minutes to blend flavors, stirring occasionally. To mixture in skillet, add okra, corn, and chicken; bring to a boil over high heat. Reduce heat to low; cover and simmer 10 to 15 minutes until vegetables are tender, stirring mixture occasionally.

Serve over warm rice.

Haitian Proverb: Ready your bed before you get sleepy.

(Prepare in advance.)

CHICKEN AND NUT STIR-FRY

Serves 4

1 lb. skinless chicken breasts cut in 1" strips	2 small onions cut in wedges (1 cup)
1 Tbs. soy sauce	2 Tbs. vegetable oil
2 tsp. cooking sherry	1 ½ Tbs. cornstarch
¼ tsp. salt	½ c. chopped cashews
1 clove garlic, crushed	¾ c. cold chicken broth or water
1 lb· fresh broccoli	

Put chicken in medium bowl with soy sauce, cooking sherry, salt and garlic; let stand for 10 minutes. Cut broccoli tops into flowerets and stems into 2" strips; set aside.

In large skillet, heat oil until hot. Add chicken mixture; stir-fry until lightly browned, 2 to 3 minutes, adding cashews at the last minute. Remove from skillet with slotted spoon draining as much oil as possible. Add onions and broccoli; stir-fry until crisp-tender, about 2 minutes.

Combine cornstarch and broth; add to vegetables. Cook and stir until slightly thickened, about 1 minute. Add cashews and reserved chicken; cook and stir 1 minute longer. Serve over steamed rice, if desired.

Variation: Add a Habanero pepper to the hot oil for about 1 minute then remove it before cooking the chicken.

ROAST CHICKEN CREOLE (WITH TWO STUFFINGS)
Serves 6

7 Tbs. butter softened	black pepper, to taste
1 garlic clove, peeled	¼ tsp. ground hot red pepper
1 c. soft fresh bread crumb	1 ½ tsp. salt
4 Tbs. lime juice	¼ tsp. ground nutmeg
1 Tbs. finely grated lime rind	½ tsp. salt
1 c. chicken stock	3 bananas, chopped fine
1 tsp. dark-brown sugar	3½-4 lb. whole roasting chicken

Preheat the oven to 350 degrees. In a heavy 6" to 8" skillet, melt 3 Tbs. of butter over moderate heat. When the foam begins to subside, drop in the garlic and stir for 10 to 15 seconds. Remove and discard the garlic; add the bread crumbs and stir until they are crisp and brown. Off the heat stir in 3 Tbs. of the lime juice, lime rind, brown sugar, nutmeg, red pepper, 1 tsp. of the salt and pepper to taste. Set this bread-crumb stuffing aside.

Put the chopped bananas into a bowl and add the remaining lime juice, ½ tsp. of salt, and pepper, and toss the ingredients with a spoon. Set aside.

Pat the chicken completely dry inside and out with paper towels. Fill the breast cavity with the banana stuffing and close the opening by lacing it with skewers or sewing it with a large needle and heavy white thread. Fill the smaller neck cavity with the bread-crumb stuffing and skewer or sew the opening shut. Truss the chicken securely and, with a pastry brush, coat it thoroughly with the 4 Tbs. of softened butter.

Place the bird on a rack in a shallow roasting pan and roast in the middle of the oven for about 1 ½ hours, basting occasionally with its own juices. Pierce the thigh of the bird. The juice that trickles out should be pale yellow; if it is tinged with pink, roast the chicken for another 5 to 10 minutes and test again.

Transfer the bird to a large, heated platter, cut off and discard the trussing strings, and let the chicken rest for about 5 minutes for easier carving. Meanwhile, skim the fat from the juices in the pan and pour in the cup of stock. Bring to a boil over high heat, stirring to the bottom of the pan. Cook the sauce briskly for 2 or 3 minutes, taste for seasoning, and pour it into a small bowl.

EASY CHICKEN CREOLE

Serves 4

1 large onion, chopped (1c.)
¾ c. diced green pepper(1 medium)
1 large clove garlic, crushed
3 Tbs. oil
2 Tbs. flour
1 can (6 oz) tomato paste
¼ tsp. hot pepper sauce
½ tsp. salt
2 c. cubed cooked chicken
¼ tsp. sugar
black pepper
hot cooked rice
2 ¼ c. chicken broth

In large skillet sauté onion, green pepper and garlic in oil until tender, stirring occasionally. Add flour; cook and stir just until flour starts to brown. Stir in tomato paste, broth, salt, sugar and pepper sauce. Cook and stir until mixture comes to boil and thickens. Simmer uncovered 5 minutes, stirring occasionally. Stir in chicken and season with black pepper. Heat until hot. Serve over hot rice.

*Haitian Proverb: When the chicken is being plucked,
the turkey doesn't laugh.*

(Don't laugh at others' misfortune, for it could hit you, too.)

CHICKEN STEW

Serves 6

1 roasting chicken (4 lb.) washed and dried
½ tsp. each salt and tarragon
¼ tsp. black pepper
5 Tbs. butter, divided
2 Tbs. oil
1 bay leaf
12 small white onions, blanched and peeled
12 small new potatoes, peeled
water
¾ c. tomato juice
2 Tbs. chopped parsley
¼ tsp. thyme
8 oz. mushrooms
1 c. artichoke hearts

Rub inside of chicken with salt, tarragon and pepper. In range top casserole large enough to hold chicken comfortably, brown chicken in 3 Tbs. butter and the oil, turning carefully to avoid breaking skin. Meanwhile in covered medium saucepan, boil onions in enough water to cover for 5 minutes. Drain; set aside. In same saucepan boil potatoes in water to cover 2 minutes, drain. Remove chicken and add onions and potatoes to the casserole; sauté, stirring gently to scrape up brown bits from bottom, until vegetables are lightly browned. Return chicken to casserole. Combine tomato juice, bay leaf, parsley and thyme; pour over chicken. Cover tightly. Bake in preheated 325 degrees oven for 30 minutes. Meanwhile in small skillet sauté mushrooms in remaining 2 Tbs. butter until lightly browned; add, with artichoke hearts, to chicken mixture. Cover tightly; bake 30 minutes longer or until chicken is tender.

WHOLE STUFFED CHICKEN

Serves 6

1 chicken
½ lb. ground veal
¼ lb. ground pork
¼ lb. sausage
¼ lb. beef tongue
¼ lb. cooked ham
¹/₈ lb. grated Parmesan
    cheese

3 slices bread soaked in milk
4 Tbs. butter
1 Tbs. pistachios
3 Tbs. brandy
2 eggs
    salt, pepper, spices (to
    taste)

Bone the chicken except for the legs, using a very sharp paring knife. Cut along the back bone of the chicken. Very carefully cut the meat away from the bones in a downwards motion. Clean and season the chicken.

Prepare the stuffing: In a bowl, mix well ground meat, sausage cut in fine pieces, eggs, cheese, bread slices (with all the milk squeezed out), salt, pepper and other spices (onion, garlic, thyme, parsley, etc.) Cut tongue and ham into strips.

Open the chicken and layer it with half of the stuffing, half of the tongue and ham strips, half of the pistachios; then repeat it once more. Close the chicken; before sewing it up, enclose the skin from the neck inside the chicken. Sew up the back and front of the chicken.

Sauté chicken in butter in a frying pan until golden. Next flame the chicken by pouring brandy into a ladle and igniting it. Pour flaming brandy over the chicken. Alcohol will burn off without flavoring the meat. Place chicken in a roasting pan and bake in 350 degree oven for 1 ½ to 2 hours, basting often.

When chicken is done, take it out of the oven and let it stand at room temperature, still in the pan, for about 10 minutes before un-sewing it. (This helps to avoid tearing the skin when un-sewing the chicken). Slice and serve with vegetables of your choice.

CHICKEN CREOLE WITH MANGO

Serves 4

3 ½ lb. broiler-fryer chicken (cut lengthwise in half
½ c. orange juice
¼ c. lemon juice
¼ c. lime juice
1 clove garlic minced
2 tsp. salt
¼ tsp. black pepper,
1 green bell pepper chopped
4 c. water
Vegetable oil

1 medium onion, peeled, cut into ½" slices
1 red bell pepper
3 Tbs. cider vinegar
2 Tbs. cornstarch
2 Tbs. tomato paste
2 Tbs. sugar
2 Tbs. water
2 mangoes, pitted, pared, cut into ½" slices
2 oranges, cut in ½" slices
3 small carrots, julienne

Combine chicken, orange juice, lemon juice, lime juice, garlic, salt and black pepper in large bowl. Let stand covered, turning occasionally, for 1 hour.

Transfer chicken mixture to large saucepan; add water and green pepper. Heat to boiling; reduce heat. Simmer covered until chicken is almost tender, about 20 minutes; remove chicken and pat dry.

Pour 6 inches oil into deep Dutch oven; heat to 375 degrees. Meanwhile, skim grease from cooking liquid; add carrots, red pepper, onion, vinegar, tomato paste and sugar. Dissolve cornstarch in water. Stir into cooking liquid. Heat until mixture thickness and bubbles for 2 minutes; reduce heat. Add mangoes and oranges; keep warm.

Fry chicken in oil until golden brown, about 10 minutes; drain on paper toweling. Transfer chicken to platter. Spoon sauce over chicken.

BELL PEPPER STEAK
Serves 6

1 ½ c. beef broth
  1 c. sliced green onions
  1 lb. lean beef, cut ½" thick
  ¼ c. each water and soy
    sauce
2 Tbs. butter or butter
  2 cloves garlic, crushed.

3 c. hot cooked rice
  2 green peppers, in strips
2 Tbs. cornstarch
  2 large fresh tomatoes,
    cut in eighths
1 Tbs. paprika

While rice is cooking, pound beef to ¼ inch thickness. Cut into ¼" wide strips. Sprinkle meat with paprika and allow to stand while preparing other ingredients. Using a large skillet, brown meat in butter. Add garlic and broth. Cover and simmer 30 minutes. Stir in onions and green peppers. Cover and cook 5 minutes more. Blend cornstarch, water, and soy sauce. Stir into meat mixture. Cook, stirring until clear and thickened, about 2 minutes. Add tomatoes and stir gently. Serve over beds of fluffy rice.

SEASONED MEAT BALLS

Mix 1 lb. ground beef with ½ lb. ground bacon or pork. Season to taste (salt, pepper, cayenne, crushed garlic) and add 3 beaten eggs. After chilling for at least one hour, shape into egg-size balls. Roll each in flour, then in beaten egg, then in bread crumbs. Deep fry or pan fry until golden. Drain. Arrange in shallow oven dish and add tomato sauce. Heat thoroughly in moderate oven. Serve very hot, with rice.

BEEF SCALOPPINE

Serves 6

1 ½ lb. beef top round steaks, cut ¼" thick	1 beef-flavor bouillon cube or envelope
1 egg	¾ c. butter or butter
3 Tbs. milk	1 garlic clove, sliced
1 ¼ c. dried bread crumbs	2 tsp. flour
¼ c. grated Parmesan cheese	¼ c. minced parsley
1 tsp. salt	$1/_8$ tsp. black pepper

Pound each beef top round steak to $1/_8$" thickness. Cut steaks into about 2" to 4" pieces.

In pie plate, beat egg with milk. On waxed paper, combine bread crumbs, Parmesan cheese, salt, and pepper. Dip meat in egg mixture, then coat with crumb mixture.

In 12" skillet over medium high heat, melt 2 Tbs. butter. Cook garlic and one-third of meat until meat is lightly browned; remove to platter; keep warm. Repeat with remaining meat, using ½ c. butter in all. In cup, mix water with flour.

Discard garlic; melt remaining butter in skillet. Add water mixture, parsley, bouillon. Cook, stirring, until thickened; pour over meat. Serve with rice and peas.

Haitian Proverb: A cow of many masters dies of hunger.

(When no one is assigned responsibility,
the job doesn't get done.)

Baked Papaya With Meat Filling

Serves 6

5 to 6 lb. green papaya cut lengthwise into halves and seeded	4 med. firm ripe tomatoes, peeled, seeded and finely chopped
3 Tbs. vegetable oil	1 tsp. finely chopped chilies
½ c. finely chopped onion	1 tsp. salt
½ tsp. finely chopped garlic	black pepper
1 lb. lean ground beef	4 Tbs. Parmesan cheese, freshly grated

Preheat the oven to 350 degrees. In a heavy 10 to 12 inch skillet, heat the oil over moderate heat until a light haze forms above it. Sauté onions and garlic until they are soft and transparent but not brown. Stir in the beef breaking it up with a fork and cook until all traces of pink disappear. Add the tomatoes (or substitute 1 ½ cups chopped, drained canned tomatoes), chilies, salt and pepper. Stirring occasionally, cook briskly until most of the liquid in the pan has evaporated and the mixture is thick enough to hold its shape almost solidly in the spoon. Taste for seasoning.

Spoon the meat mixture into the papaya shells, spreading and smoothing the filling with a spatula. Place the shells side by side in a shallow roasting pan. Pour enough boiling water in the pan to come about 1 inch up the sides of the papaya. Bake for 1 hour. Then sprinkle each shell with 1 Tbs. of the cheese and bake for 30 minutes, or until the top is delicately browned. Top shells with remaining cheese when ready to serve.

BEEF TASO

Serves 6

2 lb. boneless beef round steak cut into 1" cubes
¼ c. orange juice
¼ c. lime juice

Sauce Ti Malice (See Index)
Vegetable oil
½ Tbs. coarse salt

Combine meat, orange juice and lime juice in large bowl. Let stand covered at room temperature, stirring occasionally, 4 hours.

Transfer meat mixture to medium saucepan; add water to cover. Heat to boiling; reduce heat. Simmer covered until meat is very tender, about 1 hour. Meanwhile, make Sauce Ti Malice. Drain beef; pat dry. Heat 1½ inches oil in large skillet to 375 degrees. Fry beef, half at a time, in oil until crisp and golden brown, about 3 minutes. Remove with slotted spoon; drain on paper toweling; sprinkle with coarse salt.

Serve Taso with Sauce Ti Malice.

STIR FRY BEEF AND GREEN BEANS

1 Tbs. vegetable oil
½ c. chopped onions
1 tsp. garlic
½ lb. boneless beef

½ c. sliced mushrooms
1 c. French style green beans
2 Tbs. soy sauce
½ tsp. black pepper

Stir fry green beans in oil until tender. Remove from oil and sauté onions and garlic in oil; add beef and mushrooms and cook for 2 to 3 minutes. Then add beans, soy sauce, and pepper. Sauté for 1 minute. Serve with rice.

SURPRISE FILET

1 beef filet (2 - 4 lb.)	seasoned salt
6 strips bacon	1 clove garlic, minced
1 medium onion, sliced	1 lime, split in half
black pepper	

Rinse the filet with cool water. Rub with lime halves. Split the filet down the middle, going the entire length of the filet. Be careful to split it open and not cut it into two pieces.

Lay the filet open on counter. Place the onions, minced garlic and 3 strips of bacon along the entire length. Sprinkle with seasoned salt and pepper. Fold the filet back the way it was before splitting. Wrap the filet with the remaining strips of bacon, using toothpicks if necessary to keep in place. Let the filet marinade like this for 2 to 4 hours in refrigerator.

Remove the filet from pan and sauté in large skillet, just enough to give a little color. Remove from skillet and place in baking dish. Bake in moderate oven, 350 degrees, for 45 minutes to 1 hour or until tender. Remove toothpicks, slice diagonally in thin slices and serve hot.

Variation: Replace bacon inside filet with grated Swiss cheese.

SPICY BEEF STEW

1 lb. beef	1 clove garlic
¼ lb. bacon or ham	1 Habanero pepper
2 sweet potatoes	1 tsp. black pepper
1 yam	1 potato per person
4 tomatoes (or 1 Tbs.	½ lb. beans or chick peas
tomato paste per serving)	(soaked in advance)
1 onion	bouquet garni (spices)

Cut meat and vegetable into cubes. Add other ingredients and water to cover. Season and simmer like pot-au-feu. Serve with fried croutons.

Haitian "Court Bouillon"

2 lb. Fish fillet in pieces	1 tsp. parsley, chopped
1 Habanero pepper	1Tbs. tomato paste
1 onion, sliced	3 - 4 Tbs. cooking oil

Rub fish with lemon. Make diagonal cuts in thick pieces. Rub with salt, pepper, Habanero pepper, and chopped parsley. Add sliced onion and a few tablespoons of oil. Allow to marinate an hour or more, turning the fish so that it is thoroughly marinated.

Into the quantity of water required to come half-way up the fish, add 1 tablespoon tomato paste and 1 tablespoon flour. Put fish and marinade in pan, pour this water over them. Season to taste.

Bring to boil over low heat. Keep just under boiling. Turn the fish and continue cooking until it flakes. Do not overcook. Just before serving, add fresh butter.

New potatoes can be cooked separately and added into the court-bouillon to finish cooking. Bòy (See Index) are also a favorite addition.

Court-Bouillon A La Creole

Cut 1 lb. fish into slices, rub with lime or lemon juice and dip in flour.

2 Tbs. butter	parsley, thyme
2 Tbs. oil	2 whole cloves
2 chopped onions	1 garlic clove, crushed
1 sliced carrot (optional)	½ Habanero pepper
juice of 1 lime	1 bay leaf

Over low heat, gently brown vegetables with spices in butter and oil. Add slices of fish and just enough water to half cover the fish. Cover. Allow to poach gently 15 minutes. Turn over. Just before serving, add the juice of 1 lime or lemon.

CREOLE BOILED FISH

2 - 3 lb. fish	1 qt. boiling water
2 Tbs. vinegar or lemon juice	1 carrot, sliced
¼ c. celery leaves	1 clove garlic, sliced
4 Tbs. tomato sauce	4 whole cloves
3 onions, sliced	1 tsp. salt

Clean and wash whole fish thoroughly. Lay sliced fish in wire basket. Heat water, vegetables, and seasoning to boiling point, reduce heat and simmer for 10 minutes, add fish carefully, and simmer another 10 - 20 minutes, according to thickness of fish. Fish is done when it can be pulled from bone. Place on hot platter and garnish as desired. Serve with fish sauce.

FISH SAUCE:

1½ c. fish stock	3 Tbs. butter
2 beaten egg yolks	3 Tbs. flour
¼ c. dry white wine	salt and white pepper to taste

Melt butter, and stir in flour. Add the stock slowly, stirring constantly until sauce is thickened. Pour part of hot sauce onto egg yolks, mixing well, and then return to sauce in pan. Cook gently and stir constantly until evenly thickened, add wine, salt and white pepper to taste.

Haitian Proverb: A fish trusts the water,
but it is in water that it is cooked.

(Don't take anything for granted.)

FISH WITH ROCK SALT (PWASON GWO SÈL)

Pwason Gwo Sèl is a favorite dish at the beach. It is made with whole fish or fish filets. The best fish to use includes snapper or swordfish. The thicker the filet, the better the results. The filets should be about 1" thick.

1 lb. fish filets or whole fish	½ tsp. fresh thyme (or 1 sprig)
¼ c. fresh lime juice	¼ c. parsley, chopped
1 c. onion, thinly sliced	1 Tbl. apple cider vinegar
½ c. broth (chicken or vegetable)	6 cloves garlic, crushed
1 Habanero pepper	2 Tbl. coarse salt

Rub fish with lime juice. Place in dish and cover with broth, onion, thyme and parsley. Marinate in refrigerator for 2 - 4 hours. Bring 4 cups water, salt and vinegar to simmer. Add the Habanero pepper to the water. The pepper can be removed after a couple of minutes or left in, depending on the amount of "hotness" desired. Add fish and marinade to water and continue to simmer until fish is cooked, about 10 minutes (careful not to boil too hard or the fish will fall apart.)

Remove fish and serve. Fish is traditionally served with boiled root vegetables, such as yuca and yams. Boiled plantains are also served with this dish. Serve with Shallot Sauce or Sauce Ti Malice (See Index) for a perfect accompaniment.

BATTER FOR CHICKEN, SHRIMP, FISH, ETC.

½ lb. flour	1 tsp. baking powder
1 tsp. butter	½ tsp. ammonia powder
salt and sugar	water to make thick consistency

Mix all the above ingredients and put in the refrigerator for ½ hour or more. (If you do not have ammonia, double the quantity of baking powder.)

This batter can also be used for frying vegetables.

BAKED FISH WITH MORNAY SAUCE

Serves 4

fish filet for 4 persons	¾ c. grated Swiss cheese
1 c. white wine	4 Tbs. butter or butter
lime juice (or lemon)	2 egg yolks, beaten
white pepper	3 Tbs. flour
1 c. cream or ½ c. milk & ½	salt to taste
c. cream	

Place the filet in a baking dish, cover with white wine, cover the dish and poach the fish just until tender (do not overcook) in 325 degrees oven, about 15 - 20 minutes. When fish is cooked, remove from pan and set aside, being careful not to break it into pieces. Save the liquid.

In skillet, melt the butter and stir in the flour. Add the fish liquid to this, mixing constantly so as not to have lumps. Reduce the heat and add the cream. When this is well blended add the egg yolks. Season this mixture to taste with the lime juice, salt, and white pepper. Remove from heat and pour over fish which has been put into a baking dish.

Sprinkle top with the cheese and return to oven for 10 minutes or until hot and cheese is browned. Serve with white rice.

Haitian Proverb: When the crayfish wants to grow,
it stays in its hole.

(Avoid confrontation.)

CONCH IN CREOLE SAUCE

Serves 4

1 ½ lb. shelled conch, cleaned, skinned
2 limes, halved
3 Tbs. tomato paste
1½ tsp. minced shallots
1 tomato, peeled, seeded, chopped
3 cloves garlic, minced
¼ c. unsalted, sweet butter
1 med. onion, halved, sliced
¾ c. water
⅛ tsp. chili powder
salt and pepper to taste
1½ tsp. minced fresh thyme or ½ tsp. dried thyme
hot cooked rice

Pound conch ⅛" thick with mallet; cut into 1½" squares. Place conch in medium bowl; squeeze limes over conch. Add rinds and water to cover. Refrigerate covered 1 to 1½ hours. Drain; discard rinds.

Sauté onion, garlic and shallots in butter in Dutch oven until soft but not brown, about 5 minutes. Stir in tomato, water, tomato paste, thyme, chili powder and conch. Heat over medium heat to boiling; reduce heat to low. Simmer partially covered, stirring occasionally, until conch is fork tender, 45 - 50 minutes. Season to taste with salt and pepper.

Serve over cooked rice.

Haitian Proverb: It takes more than one finger to eat Gumbo.

(Share a little.)

CONCH STEW

Serves 6

2 lb. conch meat
½ c. white wine vinegar
1 large onion, finely chopped
1 medium green pepper, finely chopped

1 Tbs. Maggi or beef extract
3 Tbs. butter or butter
2 large tomatoes, peeled and chopped
Dash of Tabasco sauce or minced hot pepper
2 chicken bouillon cubes dissolved in ½ c. water

Clean, peel, and pound conch meat well with a wooden mallet. Then rub it with the vinegar. Cut the conch into bite size pieces.

Sauté onion and green pepper in butter. Add tomatoes, bouillon, water, Tabasco sauce, and beef extract. Simmer the stew about twenty minutes. Add conch, cover and continue to cook only until meat is tender, about ten minutes. Adjust seasonings.

CREOLE SHRIMP

Serves 6

¼ c. chopped green pepper
½ c. chopped onion
1 clove garlic, minced
3 Tbs. butter
2 c. canned tomatoes
1 - 8 oz. can tomato sauce
½ c. water
1 c. finely chopped celery

1 tsp. prepared mustard
½ tsp. sugar
dash Tabasco sauce
1 tsp. salt
$1/_8$ tsp. black pepper
1 lb. shrimp, cleaned, cooked
1 bay leaf
3 c. hot cooked rice

Sauté pepper, onion, celery, and garlic in butter. Add tomatoes, tomato sauce, water, prepared mustard, sugar, Tabasco, seasonings, and bay leaf. Simmer 20 to 25 minutes, stirring often. Add shrimp and simmer 10 minutes longer. Remove bay leaf. Serve over rice.

JAMBALAYA

Serves 8

1 c. sliced celery	1½ tsp. salt
2 c. diced green pepper	¼ tsp. Tabasco sauce
2 medium onions, chopped	2 tsp. Worcestershire sauce
4 Tbs. butter, divided	1 tsp. sugar
1 clove garlic, minced	4 c. canned tomatoes
1 lb. cooked cubed ham	½ c. canned corn, drained
1 lb. diced sausage	3 c. cooked rice
Andouille or smoked	

Cook celery, pepper, and onions in half the butter until tender, not brown. Add garlic and ham, cook 5 minutes longer. Add remaining butter, sausage, salt, Tabasco, Worcestershire, and sugar. Cook, stirring often with fork until hot. Add tomatoes, simmer uncovered about 15 minutes. Stir in rice, serve.

Variations: Shrimp or **Chicken** may be added to the recipe or substituted for the sausage.

NOTE: The origin of the name "jambalaya" is from the combination of the French word "jambon" meaning ham, the French article "à la" meaning "in the style of" and "ya," an early African word meaning rice.

Haitian Proverb: Better to be ugly but living.

(Things could be worse. Count your blessings.)

GUMBO

12 large raw shrimp	1 red pepper, chopped
1 c. crab meat	1 green pepper, chopped
4 strips bacon	6 medium tomatoes, quartered
3 Tbl. butter	½ c. celery, chopped
8 c. chicken broth	2 Tbl. parsley, chopped
1 ½ lb. okra	1 tsp. thyme
1 c. onion, chopped	4 bay leaves
4 Tbl. flour	hot sauce to taste
3 c. cooked white rice	salt and pepper to taste

In a large Dutch oven, boil shrimp in water until cooked. Remove from water and reserve liquid. Peel the shrimp and place in refrigerator until ready to use. Cook the bacon in a skillet until it just begins to take color. Remove bacon and add 2 tablespoons of the butter to bacon grease. When butter is melted, stir in the flour and make a roux. Add 2 cups of the shrimp water to this and stir until mixed and thickened. Set aside.

Discard remaining shrimp water and in Dutch oven, melt the remaining tablespoon of butter and add onion and celery. When the onions begin to turn translucent, add the okra, peppers and bacon strips and cook, stirring for another 2-3 minutes, being careful not to let this burn. Add the chicken broth and water.

Slowly add the roux, stirring so it dissolves. Add remaining ingredients, except the shrimp and crabmeat. Bring to a boil. Adjust seasonings to your liking. This is meant to be spicy, so don't be afraid to add hot sauce. Reduce heat and simmer for 1 ½ hours, stirring occasionally. Add water if needed. Mixture should be consistency of a thick stew. Add shrimp and crabmeat and simmer another 20 minutes. Stir in white rice and serve in soup bowls.

Variation: Place the rice in soup bowls and spoon the Gumbo over the rice. Substitute fish for the crab meat.

Desserts

MariBeth©

Sweet Potato Pudding (Pen Patat)

(Pen patat has a texture similar to bread pudding.)

2 lbs. white sweet potatoes	½ c. seedless raisins
2 ripe, medium bananas	1 tsp. ground cinnamon
1 c. raw (brown) sugar	1 tsp. ground ginger
2 - 12 oz. cans evaporated milk	1 tsp. vanilla extract
1 c. coconut milk	¼ tsp. ground cloves
1 Tbl. butter	¼ tsp. salt

Preheat oven to 350 degrees. Grease a 9"x13" inch cake pan.

Peel sweet potatoes and grate into mixing bowl. Mash the bananas and mix with sweet potatoes. Add the rest of the ingredients and mix well. Spread mixture evenly into cake pan.

Bake in the middle of the oven for 1½ hours, or until a cake tester or toothpick inserted in the center comes out clean and the top is golden brown. Cut into squares. May be served warm or cold.

If desired, top with whipped cream or serve with vanilla ice cream.

Flaming Bananas

Serves 4

4 ripe bananas	4 Tbl. dark rum
1/3 c. raw or brown sugar	vanilla ice cream
1/3 c. butter	

Bananas should be ripe but still firm. Peel and cut into 2" round slices. Place butter, sugar and 2 Tbl. of the rum in a non- stick skillet and heat, stirring constantly. When the syrup begins to foam, add the bananas. While stirring gently to avoid crushing, carefully ladle the boiling sauce over the banana pieces and cook for 2 minutes.

Remove from stove and group the bananas together in the middle of the pan. Pour the remaining 2 Tbl. of rum in the center and light with a torch or match. Swirl the skillet gently to move the flames over all the bananas. Spoon into serving dishes when flames subside. May be served with vanilla ice cream, if desired.

Variation: Sprinkle with 1 tsp of orange zest right before flaming.

PEANUT CAKE

1 ²/₃ c. flour	½ c. roasted ground peanuts
4 Tbs. butter	2 whole eggs
4 Tbs. sugar	pinch salt
	1 beaten egg yolk

Put flour in a medium sized mixing bowl. Make a hollow in the center and put into it the rest of the ingredients.

Knead well, roll out a few times and arrange in pie dish. Brush with beaten egg yolk.

Bake in moderate oven until knife comes out clean and cake retires from sides of mold. Sprinkle with sugar. Put under broiler a few seconds.

COCONUT PRALINES (TABLÈT KOKOYE)

2 cups coconut	2 c. raw turbinado sugar
12 oz. evaporated milk (1 can)	¼ tsp. cinnamon

There are two variations of this coconut candy. One is made with grated coconut and the other with shaved coconut. The shaved coconut version is considered fancier as it is slightly more difficult to prepare. To prepare shaved coconut run the thickness of the coconut flesh edgewise over the blade of a grater or mandoline to obtain paper thin slices about ¼ inch wide by 1 to 2 inches long.

In a saucepan combine sugar and milk. Bring to a boil and stir in the coconut. Reduce to a simmer and cook with gentle stirring until the mixture forms a thick syrup. Have a cup of ice water ready. Drop a little of the boiling syrup into it. When the syrup can be gathered up in the fingers as a soft ball, remove the saucepan from the fire.

Spoon the candy onto a greased cookie sheet into rough circles about 3 inches wide. Leave room between the pralines (tablèt) to allow room for some crawl as they cool. Allow the pralines to cool completely before lifting them. Store in an airtight container.

Variations: Besides the different ways the coconut can be prepared, excellent tablèt is also made using peanuts or cashew nuts instead of coconut.

CARROT CAKE

4 eggs	2 tsp. cinnamon
2 c. grated carrots	2 c. sugar
3 c. sifted flour	1 tsp. baking soda
1 c. chopped nuts	1 tsp. salt
3 tsp. baking powder	¼ tsp. nutmeg
½ c. raisins	1¼ tsp. ginger
	1½ c. oil

Mix eggs and carrots. Add sugar gradually, then chopped nuts and raisins. Sift dry ingredients together, including spices, and add to mixture. Add oil. Bake in 13 x 9 x 2 inch pan at 350 degrees for 30 - 35 minutes. Ice with cream cheese icing.

Cream Cheese Icing:

1 pkg. cream cheese, 8 oz	2 tsp. vanilla
¼ c. butter	1 c. chopped nuts
1 lb. confectioners sugar	

Work cheese until soft. Add softened butter. Beat in sugar gradually. Add flavoring and nuts. Mix and spread.

MANGO COFFEE CAKE

½ c. butter or butter	1 tsp. soda
1½ c. sugar	½ c. buttermilk or sour milk
2 eggs	1 tsp. vanilla
2 c. sifted flour	½ c. chopped nuts
½ tsp. salt	juice of one lime or lemon
1½ tsp. baking powder	½ c. confectioners sugar
1½ c. mango pulp	

Cream shortening; add sugar gradually, cream until fluffy. Beat in eggs one at a time. Add mango pulp and beat well. Sift together dry ingredients. Add alternately with milk. Add vanilla and blend. Add nuts, turn into a 11 ½" x 7 ½" pan or two 8" layer pans greased and floured. Bake 350 degrees for 25 - 35 minutes. Glaze with juice of 1 lime/lemon and ½ c. confectioners' sugar.

BUTTERY-ORANGE RAISIN CAKE

4 c. flour	¼ tsp. almond extract
2 tsp. baking powder	2 c. raisins
½ tsp. salt	1 ½ c. milk
2 tsp. baking soda	2 Tbs. vinegar
2½ c. sugar	4 eggs
juice from 2 oranges	1 c. butter
(reserve rinds and 6	
Tbs. juice)	

Sift first 4 ingredients. Combine ½ c. orange juice and ½ c. sugar until sugar is dissolved. Add extract. Refrigerate.

Grind reserved rind and add to raisins. Combine together milk and vinegar. Cream butter and beat in rest of sugar. Add eggs, one at a time. Add the rest of the ingredients gradually. Pour into pan.

Bake 60 to 70 minutes. Remove from oven and spoon 6 tablespoons reserved orange juice over the top and between cake and sides of pan. Return cake to turned-off oven for 1 hour.

MANGO ICE CREAM PIE

1 baked pie shell or	1 small pkg. peach
graham cracker crust	gelatin
1 pt. vanilla ice cream	1½ c. chopped mango

Drain fruit and to juice add enough hot water to make 1 cup liquid. Dissolve gelatin in hot liquid and add ice cream. Stir until dissolved and refrigerate until becomes the consistency of egg white. Then add fruit and pour into a pie shell and refrigerate.

MOCK APPLE PIE

6 chayote (militon)
1½ c. sugar
4 Tbs. flour
1 Tbs. lime juice
the tartness makes the
militon taste even more
like apples)

1 tsp. cinnamon
¼ tsp. nutmeg
dash salt
unbaked pie shell

Boil the chayote until done. Peel and cut into pieces resembling sliced apples. Combine all ingredients except the chayote. Lightly toss the chayote with this mixture. Line a 9 inch pie pan with pastry and fill with the chayote mixture. Mix together the following:

TOPPING

½ c. sugar
1/3 c. butter

½ c. flour

Sprinkle over pie and bake at 400 degrees for 40 minutes or until bubbly and golden.

NOTE: 4 c. thinly sliced grenadines may be used in place of the chayote.

MANGO PIE

6 - 8 half ripe mangoes
2/3 c. sugar
2 Tbs. flour

2 tsp. lime juice
1 Tbs. cinnamon
1 unbaked pie shell

Make a rich pie crust. Peel mangoes and slice very thin. Mix with other ingredients. Top with bits of butter. Cover or criss-cross with pie crust. Bake about 40 minutes at 350 degrees.

Sweet Potato Pie

5 medium white sweet potatoes (patat)	½ c. white or brown sugar firmly packed
4 eggs, slightly beaten	$1/_8$ tsp. nutmeg
1 tsp. rum extract	grating of fresh ginger
½ tsp. allspice	1½ c. light cream
½ tsp. salt	1 tsp. cinnamon

Peel and dice sweet potatoes into cubes. Simmer them in salted water until tender. Drain and mash the sweet potatoes, removing any lumps. Add to the mashed sweet potatoes the eggs, brown sugar, salt, and spices and mix well. Add cream and extract. Spoon the mixture into Windward Island Pie Crust shell (below). Bake for an hour, or until the custard is set and a knife inserted in the filling is clean when withdrawn.

Windward Island Pie Crust

(Makes one deep 10" pie crust)

¾ c. butter	4 c. flour
¾ c. sugar	1 tsp. baking powder
1 egg	¼ tsp. salt
3 Tbs. cold water	

Preheat oven to 350 degrees. Cream butter and sugar. Beat egg and add to butter mixture. Sift and mix dry ingredients.

Stir the dry ingredients into the butter and egg mixture and then knead the dough on a lightly floured surface. It should remain soft and spongy. If the dough seems heavy, sprinkle it lightly with water and knead it a second time. Pat the pastry into place, leaving a generous over-hang of dough around the rim of the pie pan. This is later folded over the filling to make a wide band of top crust around the edge of the pie. Place filling (see above) in the pastry shell, and brush the top crust with egg, well beaten.

Cover the pie tightly with aluminum foil and place it in the pre-heated oven. Remove the foil fifteen minutes later, but continue baking the pie an additional half-hour, or until the crust is golden.

LIME PIE

Serve 6

1 Tbs. unflavored gelatin	$1/_8$ tsp. salt
¼ c. cold water	2-3 tsp. grated lime peel
4 eggs, separated	Green food coloring
1 c. sugar, divide	1 baked, 9" pie shell
$1/_3$ c. lime juice	½ c. heavy cream, whipped

Soften gelatin in cold water. Beat egg yolks, add ½ cup sugar, lime juice, and salt. Cook over hot water stirring constantly, until thickened. Add lime peel and gelatin. Stir until gelatin is dissolved and add food coloring to tint a soft pale green. Cool. Beat egg whites until stiff, adding remaining sugar slowly. Fold into lime mixture. Pour into pie shell, chill until firm. Garnish with whipped cream or meringue.

COCONUT CREAM PIE

1 baked 9-inch pie shell	3 egg yolks, beaten
$1/_3$ c. sugar	1 Tbs. butter
2 Tbs. cornstarch	1 tsp. vanilla
$1/_8$ tsp. salt	¾ c. grated coconut
1½ c. scalded milk	2 Tbs. dark rum (optional)

Meringue: 2 egg whites and 4 Tbs. sugar

Preheat oven to 300 degrees. Add $1/_3$ cup sugar, cornstarch, and salt to egg yolks. Pour milk into this, place in double boiler, stir and cook until thickened. Add rum and cook about 1 minute more, stirring constantly. Add butter, coconut, and vanilla. Pour into pie shell. Beat egg whites until foamy; gradually add sugar. Beat until mixture stands in peaks. Pile lightly on cooled pie. Place in oven to brown. (If desired sprinkle top with toasted coconut.)

Variation: 1 tsp. rum flavoring may be substituted for the rum.

RICE PUDDING

2 c. rice - precooked	½ c. brown sugar
1 tsp. cinnamon	½ tsp. nutmeg
½ tsp. allspice	½ tsp. ginger
½ tsp. salt	1 c. milk
½ tsp. cloves	1 Tbs. vanilla
½ c. raisins, nuts	2 eggs beaten

Combine all ingredients and bake for 30 minutes at 350 degrees.

COCONUT PUDDING

2 medium coconuts	1 Tbs. grated lime peel
½ c. water	½ c. water
1 can (14 oz) sweetened condensed milk	2 envelopes unflavored gelatin
1 can (13 oz) evaporated milk	1 tsp. vanilla
1¼ c. water	$1/_8$ tsp. salt

Pierce eyes of coconuts with an ice pick or nail. Strain coconut water and measure 1 ¾ cups; add ½ cup water; reserve. Heat condensed milk, evaporated milk and 1¼ cups water in medium saucepan to boiling. Soften gelatin in ½ c. water. Add to milk mixture, stirring until gelatin dissolves. Stir in reserved coconut water, the lime peel, vanilla and salt. Pour into large serving bowl. Refrigerate covered until set, about 4 hours. Garnish with shredded coconut and maraschino cherries, if desired.

BANANA FRITTERS (BENYEN)

4 ripe bananas	¼ c. sugar
4 Tbl. white flour	½ tsp. baking soda
½ tsp. cinnamon powder	2 c. corn oil
1 tsp. vanilla extract	powdered sugar

Mix ingredients in a bowl or food processor. Heat oil to frying temperature. Spoon batter into hot oil and fry until golden brown. Drain well and sprinkle with powdered sugar while still hot.

GRANNY'S PEANUT BRITTLE

1 c. sugar	¾ tsp. baking soda
1 c. corn syrup	½ tsp. salt
2 c. raw peanuts	½ tsp. cinnamon
1 Tbs. water	

Grease 2 cookies sheets.

Combine sugar, syrup, and water. Let boil a few minutes then put in peanuts and cook until the peanuts almost stop popping. Take off fire and quickly stir in soda, salt, and cinnamon. Spread thinly on well greased pans and when cool break pieces and put in covered containers.

COCONUT FUDGE (DOUS KOKOYE)

1 lb. brown sugar	1 lb. grated coconut
1 c. water	½ tsp. lime juice

In a saucepan combine brown sugar and water. Simmer gently until mixture forms a thick syrup. Have a cup of cold water ready. Drop a little of the boiling syrup into it. When the syrup can be gathered up in the fingers as a soft ball, remove the saucepan from the fire. Stir in immediately coconut and lime juice. Turn out onto a lightly buttered platter and spread to cool.

PLANTAIN PUDDING (LABOUYI)

2 green plantains	½ c. sugar
2 ripe bananas	2 cinnamon sticks
1 can (12 oz) coconut milk	2 whole star anise pods
1 can (12 oz) evaporated milk	1 tsp. vanilla extract

Boil the plantains until tender (about 20 minutes). Blend the plantains with the bananas, sugar, evaporated milk and coconut milk. Add the cinnamon and star anise and cook for 15 minutes. Remove the cinnamon and star anise. Serve warm. If desired, add milk and sugar to taste.

PECAN PEACH CREPES

Serves 8

6 oz. cream cheese, softened	29 oz. can peach slices
3 Tbs. sugar	2 Tbs. cornstarch
2 Tbs. milk	½ c. orange juice
½ tsp. grated orange peel	2 Tbs. lemon juice
½ tsp. vanilla	2 Tbs. butter or butter
16 dessert crepes (recipe below)	¼ c. finely chopped nuts

For filling: Blend cream cheese, sugar, milk, orange peel, and vanilla.

To Assemble: Spoon filling in center of unbrowned side of crepe; sprinkle with nuts. Fold crepe in half; fold in half again, forming a triangle. Repeat with remaining crepes. Drain peach slices; reserve syrup. In chafing dish or skillet blend syrup into cornstarch. Add orange juice, lemon juice, and butter. Cook and stir until thickened and bubbly. Add peaches. Spoon sauce over crepes; heat through.

DESSERT CREPES

1 c. all purpose flour	2 Tbs. sugar
1½ c. milk	1 Tbs. oil
2 eggs	¼ tsp. salt

In bowl combine flour, milk, eggs, sugar, oil, and salt; beat with rotary beater until blended. Heat a lightly greased 6 inch skillet. Remove from heat. Spoon in 2 Tbs. batter; lift and tilt skillet to spread batter. Return to heat; brown on one side. Invert pan over paper toweling; remove crepe. Repeat to make 16 to 18 crepes, greasing skillet each time.

FLAN
Serves 4

1/3 c. sugar	1/4 c. sugar
2 beaten eggs	1 tsp. vanilla
13 oz. can evaporated milk	dash salt

In small skillet heat and stir the 1/3 cup sugar over medium heat until sugar melts and becomes golden brown. Quickly pour the sugar mixture into a 3½ cup ring mold or four 6 oz. custard cups, tilting to coat bottom and sides.

Combine eggs, evaporated milk, ¼ cup sugar, vanilla, and salt. Pour into caramel coated mold or cups; set in baking pan on oven rack. Pour hot water around mold or cups in pan to depth of one inch. Bake in a 325 degree oven for 50 to 55 minutes (35 to 40 for custard cups) or until knife inserted halfway between center and edge comes out clean. Chill. Loosen custard from sides; if necessary place custard dish in hot water for a few seconds. Invert onto platter or serving plates.

CARROT PIE
Serves 6-8

¾ c. sugar	3 large eggs, lightly beaten
1 tsp. ginger	1 c. milk
1 tsp. cinnamon	½ tsp. vanilla
¼ tsp. salt	pastry for 9" pie
1 tsp. nutmeg	
2 c. mashed cooked carrots	

Preheat oven to 400 degrees. Combine sugar, spices, and salt in mixing bowl. Add carrots and eggs, mix well. Stir in milk and vanilla. Pour mixture in pie shell and bake for 40 to 50 minutes or until firm. Cool before serving.

FRUIT SHERBET

Serves 16 (makes 2 quarts)

1 ¾ lb. fresh ripe fruit (melon,
    papaya, mango, guava)
4 c. milk
2 env. unflavored gelatin
¾ tsp. salt

3 drops yellow food color
    (or color of fruit, optional)
½ c. sugar
¾ c. light corn syrup

Peel and seed fruit. Cut into chunks. In covered blender at medium speed or in food processor with knife blade attached, blend fruit (you may use any fruit of your choice) and 1 cup milk until smooth; set aside.

In 3-quart saucepan, sprinkle the 2 envelopes of gelatin evenly over 1 cup milk. Cook over medium-low heat until gelatin is completely dissolved, stirring constantly. Remove saucepan from heat; stir in fruit mixture, remaining milk, corn syrup, and remaining ingredients. (Mixture may have curdled appearance.) Pour mixture into 13" x 9" baking pan. Cover with foil and freeze until partially frozen, about 3 hours, stirring occasionally.

Spoon mixture into chilled large bowl; with mixer at medium speed, beat until smooth but still frozen. For smooth sherbet you must keep the fruit mixture frozen while you beat it, so it's best if you chill the mixing bowl and beaters in the freezer for a while. (If the mixture melts, ice crystals may form, resulting in a coarse, icy texture).

Repeat as before, with beating mixture. Return mixture to pan. Cover and freeze until firm, about 3 hours.

MOLASSES CINNAMON GINGERBREAD (BONBON SIWO)

4 c. flour	2 tsp. ground cinnamon
½ tsp. baking powder	½ tsp. ground cloves
½ tsp. baking soda	½ c. butter, softened
½ tsp. salt	½ c. raw sugar (turbinado)
2 tsp. ground ginger	1 c. molasses
	¾ c. hot water

Preheat oven to 350 degrees. Sift together the flour, sugar, salt, baking powder, baking soda, and spices. Stir in the butter and molasses. Slowly pour half the hot water over the dough while stirring vigorously. Gradually add water until the dough is soft to the touch but not sticky like a batter. Depending on the humidity of your flour you may not need all of the water or may need to add a bit of flour for the correct consistency.

Press the mixed dough evenly into a greased and floured 9" x 13" cake pan. Using a table knife, score the top of the dough into more or less 24 squares depending on portion size preference.

Bake for 30 to 40 minutes, until the cake springs back when lightly pressed with a finger.

NOTE: For a fuller flavor, make the day before using, cover and let stand at room temperature until serving. The flavors of the molasses and ginger become more intense as the gingerbread ages.

Variation: To enhance the ginger flavor, use ground fresh ginger in place of powdered ginger.

*Haitian Proverb: Every bread has its oven
as well as its cheese.*

(Everyone has trials and joys, and every trial has its joy.)

FRUIT CAKE DELIGHT

For 2 loaf pans, approximately 10"x 4"x 5"

3 c. sifted flour
1 tsp. baking powder
¼ tsp. salt (if using unsalted butter)
1½ tsp. powdered cinnamon
½ tsp. powdered cloves
1 tsp. powdered nutmeg
1 c. butter
½ c. Mango chutney (Recipe Index)

6 beaten eggs
½ c. orange juice
2 c. blanched ground almonds
1½ c. cashew nuts
½ c. peanuts
½ c. candied pineapple
½ c. candied orange
1 box currants or raisins

Thoroughly mix flour, baking powder, salt and spices and sift three times. Beat butter until smooth and light, add in sugar gradually, then while still beating slowly, add eggs, juice, nuts, chutney, candied fruit and finally the flour.

Pour into buttered loaf pans lined with buttered paper. Bake in slow oven (300 degrees) about two hours. In small molds, bake about 25 minutes. Remove paper and cool on rack.

NOTE: This recipe can be made with or without the chutney. The chutney gives it more of a pudding texture.

CROUTONS

(Stale French bread makes excellent croutons)

For flavored croutons that go with any Creole meal, make a mixture of softened butter, freshly squeezed garlic and a little thyme. Butter slices of stale bread and cut into crouton sized pieces. Either sauté in skillet or bake in slow oven until crisp and light brown.

Variation: Plain croutons can be made by cutting bread in pieces and baking in a slow oven, turning occasionally, until light brown and crisp.

Variation: Try other flavors such as a little grated Parmesan cheese. Or for a zesty crouton sprinkle with Pepper Sauce (See Index) before sautéing.

MAYONNAISE

1 egg yolk	pinch of salt
1 c. oil	black pepper to taste
1 Tbs. vinegar or lemon juice	mustard to taste
1 Tbs. boiling water	

Blend egg yolk, salt, pepper, mustard and vinegar until quite smooth in a blender. Add oil, first very slowly, almost drop by drop, then, as the sauce thickens, in larger quantities (one tablespoon at a time) until the sauce is quite firm.

While still beating, add in 1 tablespoon boiling water, which makes the sauce more digestible, lighter and more stable. It can be kept in the refrigerator a week or two.

Haitian Proverb: Memory is a sieve.

(It's easy to forget things.)

PIKLIZ RELISH

8 oz. shredded cabbage	2 thinly sliced Habanero peppers
1 oz. shredded carrot	¼ c. fresh lime juice
1 oz. shredded turnip	¼ c. white vinegar
1 oz. thinly sliced shallots	2 tsp. salt

Pikliz is the relish of Haiti. It is considered that good pikliz makes any savory food taste better.

Shred the vegetables into very thin slices 2 to 3 inches long. Mix them and sprinkle the salt over them in a non-metallic container. Remove the seeds from the Habanero peppers, slice them into thin circle slices, and place them into the freshly squeezed lime juice. Firmly pack the vegetables into a glass jar alternating layers of vegetables and a few slices of pepper and lime juice. Top off the jar with white vinegar to cover the vegetables.

Cover the jar and allow it to pickle for at least 4 hours. Pikliz is at its peak after 1 or 2 days of pickling. If kept more than one day it should be refrigerated.

SIMPLIFIED WHITE BUTTER

(To serve with hot fish, preferably broiled or baked)

2 Tbs. finely chopped shallots	¼ c. white wine vinegar
1 Tbs. coarse salt	1 Tbs. water
black pepper	½ c. butter

In a large pan (to facilitate evaporation), combine first five ingredients. (Onions may be substituted for shallots.) Boil. In a small bowl, soften butter.

When the liquid in the pan has boiled down to 1 Tbs. remove from heat and add into butter, stirring vigorously. Keep in refrigerator. Serve with hot fish.

PEPPER SAUCE (SÒS PIMAN)

2 Habanero peppers	½ c. fresh lime juice
1 Tbs. salt	½ c. white vinegar

Remove and discard the seeds from the Habanero peppers. Blend the peppers thoroughly with the other ingredients in a food processor or blender. Pour the sauce into a bottle with care as it will have strong fumes when it first comes out of the blender. Store the sauce in the refrigerator and allow it to stand for 24 hours before use. Peak flavors will develop after about a week.

This sauce is intensely flavorful. A few drops will enhance the flavor of savory dishes. The combination of the fresh lime juice with the Habanero peppers develops unique complex aromatic fruitlike flavors unlike those found in other chilies. The heat intensity can be adjusted by increasing or decreasing the number of peppers.

DUMPLINGS (BÒY)

Light dumplings:

1 c. flour	pinch salt
2 Tbs. baking powder	2 Tbs. butter
cold water	

Cut butter into flour until it forms pea-sized lumps. Gradually add water until consistency is like that of a non-sticky pizza dough. Form into finger like shapes.

Cook in gravy, soup or salted boiling water 5 to 10 minutes.

Chewy dumplings:

Omit baking powder and butter. Use hot water instead of cold. Cook at least 20 minutes in salted water, meat or fish sauce, soups or with Sòs Pwa (See Index).

Mango Chutney

5 c. mango pulp, cut into
slices, - (the Francique
variety)

4 c. sugar   2 c. vinegar
1 Tbs. powdered cloves   Salt (optional)
¼ c. raisins (optional)   1 Tbs. powdered cinnamon

Put spices into small cheese cloth sachet (or piece of nylon hose.)
Pour vinegar and sugar over them and cook into syrup. Put
mango pulp into syrup, bring to boil and after 10 minutes reduce
heat and allow to simmer 2 hours. Put into jars.

Variation: Add ¼ cup raisins just before removing from heat.

Guava Jelly

Peel, remove seeds and cut the guavas into pieces. Cook until
very tender in water, about to 210 degrees on a candy
thermometer. Put fruit through a sieve and strain to where you
only have pure juice. Be careful not to press fruit, as the juice will
become bitter.

Add one cup sugar to each cup of guava juice. Bring again to a
boil and add for each cup of juice 1 teaspoon lime juice. Cook
only 4 cups at a time.

Coconut Jam

Grate 1 coconut. Make a syrup with 1 cup water, 1 cup sugar and
1 teaspoon vanilla. Add grated coconut. Cook ½ hour over low
heat, stirring occasionally. When coconut pulp is transparent,
remove from heat and mix in gently 2 eggs yolks. Cool. Serve
with bread, or use to fill a pre-baked pie shell. Place pie shell in
moderate oven for 10 minutes.

Spicy Peanut Butter (Manba)

1 jar natural peanut butter   ¼ Habanero pepper, no seeds

Chop Habanero pepper into small pieces and blend or process with 2 – 3 tablespoons of peanut butter. When well blended, stir and mix well into remaining peanut butter. Traditionally, country peanut butter in Haiti is spiced with hot pepper. It goes well with casava bread (See Index).

Tomato Jam

Plunge tomatoes into boiling water a few seconds, then into iced water. Skins will burst and are easily removed. Press tomatoes to eliminate juice. Cut pulp into pieces and measure. Per 4 cups pulp, measure 2 cups sugar and 1 thinly sliced lemon (or lime).

Cook tomato pulp and lemon slices until skin of lemon is tender (30 to 40 minutes) over low heat. Add sugar and continue cooking and stirring 15 minutes more.

Mock Applesauce

Cut into small pieces:

6 chayotes (militons)
½ c. lime juice

1 apple or green mango
sugar, salt, cinnamon to taste

Cut and simmer chayotes and apple or mango in a very little water until soft, remove skins, then beat with blender until like applesauce. Add ½ cup lime juice and a little salt, sugar, and cinnamon to taste.

Coconut Milk

Pour 3 c. boiling water over 1 c. grated (unsweetened) coconut. Cover tightly and infuse (like tea) for thirty minutes. Pour liquid through a fine sieve, pressing all the moisture from the coconut. Discard the coconut, as it is now tasteless.

GREEN PLANTAIN CHIPS

2 Cups

Vegetable oil or	1 large plantain
shortening for frying	(about 1 lb.)
Salt	

Peel plantain skin as shown (See Index). With your fingers pull the skin away from the white banana-like fruit inside and pull or cut off the fibrous strings. Slice the plantain crosswise into paper-thin rounds.

Fill a deep fryer or large, heavy saucepan with vegetable oil or shortening to a depth of 2 or 3 inches and heat to a temperature of 375 degrees on a deep-frying thermometer.

Deep-fry the plantain slices, a dozen or so at a time, for 3 or 4 minutes, turning them with a slotted spoon until they are golden brown on both sides. As they brown, transfer them to paper towels to drain.

Sprinkle with salt and serve the chips warm or at room temperature.

GRANOLA

Makes 4 quarts

½ c. oil	½ tsp. salt
½ lb. butter or butter	2 lb. rolled oats
2 Tbs. molasses	1 c. chopped nuts
1 Tbs. vanilla	1 lb. coconut
1 c. brown sugar	1 c. raisins
1 c. honey	1 c. dried fruit (optional)

Preheat oven to 350 degrees. Melt first seven ingredients in roasting pan. When mixed, let cool slightly. Add the rest of ingredients except for the raisins and dried fruit. Stir thoroughly. Bake in shallow pans or on cookie sheets for 20 - 25 minutes. Stir every 5 - 7 minutes. After granola has cooled, add raisins and dried fruit. Store in tightly covered container.

HELPFUL HINTS

How To Handle Chilies

Hot peppers, especially Habanero peppers, require special handling. Their volatile oils may burn your skin and make your eyes smart. Wear rubber gloves if you can, and be careful not to touch your face or eyes while working with chilies.

To prepare Habanero peppers, rinse them clean and pull out the stems under cold running water. Break or cut the pods in half, and brush out the seeds with your fingers. In most cases the ribs inside the pods are thin and may be left intact, but if they seem fleshy, cut them out with a small, sharp knife. The chilies may be used at once or soaked in cold, salted water for an hour or so to make them less hot.

Be sure to wash your hands thoroughly with soap and warm water after handling hot chilies.

How To Peel A Green Plantain

Ripe plantains can be peeled as easily as bananas. But the green ones used for plantains chips or for BANNANN PEZE require special handling, since the thick skin clings tightly to the fruit and tends to break off in little pieces. The diagram below illustrates an efficient and unfrustrating way of removing the peel. With a sharp knife, slice off the ends and cut the plantain in half. Make four evenly spaced lengthwise slits in the skin of each half, cutting through to the flesh from one end to the other. Then, starting at the corner edge of one slit, lift the skin away a strip at a time - pulling if off crosswise rather than lengthwise.

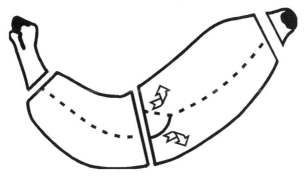

COOKING HINTS

1. Raw cane syrup can be substituted for corn syrup in recipes and has good nutritional value. In Haiti, it can be purchased in bulk in the market. Send your own bottle. Before using, strain and boil for 10 minutes.

2. When cooking white rice, a little lime juice added will whiten and fluff it.

3. To make confectioners' icing sugar, put 1 cup granulated sugar and 1 tsp. cornstarch together in a blender. Blend about 1 minute until powdered.

4. Homemade brown sugar can be made by adding 2 tablespoons molasses to 1 cup white sugar. More molasses may be added if you want darker sugar.

5. Haitian meat tenderizing method: Crush a papaya leaf in your hand and with a little water, rub thoroughly all over meat. Cook or rinse meat within the hour to avoid over tenderizing.

6. Green mangoes, militon, green papaya, and grenadine are all good substitutes in recipes calling for apples. If the fruit seems to lack tartness and flavor add a little salt and lime juice to the recipe.

7. Zucchini squash can be substituted for cucumbers in making bread and butter pickles.

8. Flours vary widely in moisture content. A good practice with any kneaded bread is to reserve the last cup to add as necessary, a little at a time, during kneading.

9. When you find mold on your cheese, just trim off the mold and use remaining cheese - it's perfectly safe.

10. Grate hard, dry cheese finely and sprinkle over spaghetti or other dishes.

Cooking Hints (Cont.)

11. If you have leftover egg yolks, cover unbroken yolks with water to prevent drying out in the refrigerator.

12. Use extra egg yolks to enrich scrambled eggs, fried rice, breads, cakes, cookies, etc.

13. Crumb crust - Crumb together 1 cup flour, ¼ cup brown sugar and ½ cup butter. Spread on cookie sheet and bake at 350 degrees, turning often until golden. Crush fine before lining baking dish.

14. In Haiti, whole wheat can be hard to find. Bulgur from the market can be cooked slightly and added to bread dough during the kneading for added taste and texture.

15. To blanch almonds, put them into a saucepan and cover with cold water. Bring to a boil, strain them and run cold water over them. Then dry them in a cloth. The skins will slip off easily.

16. A well beaten egg white added to mashed potatoes will add to the looks and taste of the dish.

17. Lemon juice or vinegar in the water cauliflower is cooked in makes it keep its snowy white color.

18. A fork should never be stuck into a steak or chop that is being fried or grilled, because it lets the juice out.

19. Grate a raw potato and add it to your soup when you put too much salt in it. The potato absorbs the salt.

20. Use the divider from an ice tray to cut biscuits in a hurry. Shape dough to conform with size of divider and cut. After baking, biscuits will separate at dividing lines.

Cooking Hints (Cont.)

21. To strain cooking oil after deep-fat frying, place a paper coffee filter in the funnel used to put the oil back into its bottle. Then just throw the filter and crumbs away.

22. Leftover rice? Don't toss out. Save and reheat next day. Place it into a large strainer, set over simmering water, cover and steam until fluffy and hot.

23. Freeze leftover cornbread for use in stuffings.

24. Dice untoasted stale bread to use in meat loaves. A blender quickly turns bread pieces into crumbs.

25. Whirl small amounts of leftover dishes in the blender and incorporate resulting sauce into another soup or main dish.

26. Save all bones and meat scraps for making soups.

27. When serving something "flambée" or "flaming," a small amount of alcohol such as rum or brandy will produce a larger flame if poured into one spot in the pan or dish (rather than sprinkled over the whole dish). With a little swirling motion, the flames can be moved to cover the dish.

28. Out of eggs or can't eat them? Substitute eggs with a butter and a little thickening agent like tapioca flour or corn starch. Use 2 Tsp. thickner and 1 Tbl. butter for one egg. (This does not work in pudding or custard.)

ABBREVIATIONS COMMONLY USED

tsp.- teaspoon

Tbs.- Tablespoon

c.- cup

pt.- pint

qt.-quart

doz.- dozen

oz.- ounce or ounces

lb.- pound or pounds

sq.- square

min.- minute or minutes

hr.- hour or hours

med.- medium

EQUIVALENT MEASURES AND WEIGHTS

3 teaspoons = 1 tablespoon

4 tablespoons = ¼ cup

16 tablespoons = 1 cup

1 cup = ½ pint

2 cups = 1 pint

2 pints (4 cups) =1 quart

4 quarts = 1 gallon

16 ounces = 1 pound

* If you want to measure part-cups by the tablespoon, remember:

4 Tbs. = ¼ cup

5 1/3 Tbs. = $^1/_3$ cup

8 Tbs. = ½ cup

10 $^2/_3$ Tbs. - $^2/_3$ cups

12 Tbs. = ¾ cup

14 Tbs. = $^7/_8$ cup

OVEN TEMPERATURES

Slow..300 degrees

Slow moderate...325 degrees

Moderate... 350 degrees

Quick moderate... 375 degrees

Moderately hot.. .400 degrees

Hot..425 degrees

Very hot...475 degrees

METRIC CONVERSION

WEIGHT

1	kilogram	=	1000	grams
1	kilogram	=	2-½	pounds
1	milligram		.0001	gram
1	gram	=	1/30	ounce
1	ounce	=	approx.	30 grams
1	pound	=	approx.	450 grams
1	cup	=	approx.	200 grams butter (or liquid solids)
1	cup	=	approx.	200 grams sugar or granular foods
1	cup	=	approx.	125 grams flour (or fine powders)
1	cup	=	approx.	200 grams rice (or grains)

VOLUME

1	centiliter	=	.01	liter
1	milliliter	=	.001	liter
1	liter	=	1 1/16	quarts
1	quart	=	.95	liter
1	fluid ounce	=	30	ml.
1	tablespoon	=	15	ml.
1	teaspoon	=	5	ml.
1	cup	=	230	ml.

SUBSTITUTIONS AND EQUIVALENTS

1 tsp. Baking powder	¼ tsp. baking soda plus ½ tsp. cream or tartar
1 lb. kidney beans, dry	9 cups cooked
1 lb. lima beans, dry	6 cups cooked
1 lb. navy beans, dry	6 cups cooked
$1/_3$ cup bread crumbs, dry	1 slice
¾ cup bread crumbs, soft	1 slice
1 cup butter	1 cup margarine
1 cup butter	$4/_5$ cup bacon fat, clarified
1 cup butter	¾ cup chicken fat, clarified
1 cup butter	$7/_8$ cup oil or lard
1 cup buttermilk	1 cup yogurt
1 square (1 oz.) chocolate	3 Tbs. cocoa plus 1 Tbs. fat
3 ½ oz. coconut, fine grated	1 cup grated coconut
5 cup coconut, shredded	1 lb. shredded coconut
40 cups coffee	1 lb. coffee.
25 servings coffee, instant	2 oz. jar
3 cups cornmeal	1 lb. cornmeal.
1 cup cornmeal, cooked	4 c. cooked cornmeal
1 Tbs. cornstarch	2 Tbs. flour or 1 ½ Tbs. quick cooking tapioca
1 cup cream, heavy	$2/_3$ cup milk and $1/_3$ cup butter
1 cup cream, whipped	$2/_3$ cup well- chilled evaporated milk, whipped

SUBSTITUTIONS AND EQUIVALENTS (CONT.)

1 cup cream, sour	$^1/_3$ cup butter ¾ cup sour milk
1 cup flour, cake	2 Tbs. cornstarch in cup; fill with white flour and sift 3 times
1 cup flour, all-purpose	1 cup plus 2 Tbs. cake flour
1 garlic clove	$^1/_8$ tsp. garlic powder or ¼ tsp. garlic salt: reduce $^1/_8$ tsp. salt
1 Tbs. raw ginger	$^1/_8$ tsp. ginger powder
1 Tbs. fresh herbs	1 tsp. dried herbs or ¼ tsp. powdered herbs or ½ tsp. herb salt: reduce salt ¼ tsp.
1 cup honey	1 cup molasses or ¾ sugar plus ¼ tsp. liquid
1 cup sugar	1 cup honey, reduce other liquid ¼ cup. Reduce baking temp. 25 degrees
1 cup macaroni, uncooked	2 to 2 ¼ cup cooked
1 cup milk	4 Tbs. powdered milk and 1 cup water
1 cup milk	½ cup evaporated milk and ½ cup water
1 cup milk, sour	1 Tbs. lemon or vinegar and enough sweet milk to measure 1 cup
1 cup noodles, uncooked	1 ¾ cup cooked
1 med. onion	2 Tbs. instant minced onion or 1 tsp. onion powder or 2 tsp. onion salt: reduce salt 1 tsp.
1 cup rice, uncooked	2 cup rice, cooked
1 cup sugar	1 cup honey; reduce other liquid ¼ cup; reduce baking temp. 25 degrees

COMMON FOOD NAMES TRANSLATED

ENGLISH	FRENCH	CREOLE	DESCRIPTION AND USE
Acerola	Cerise	Seriz	Small pumpkin shaped, crimson colored "cherries". Used for beverage. Put in blender; sweeten, Make into preserves.
Almond	Amande	Zanmann	Tropical "Almond" has a bitter yellow fruit covering the nut inside. Break open to eat nut.
Apple	Pomme	Pòm	Sour and very acid. Used in pies and jellies.
Apricot	Abricot	Zabriko	Large round brown skin tropical "apricot:". Pulp is orange and firm with 2-3 large pits. Can be eaten fresh, in salads or stewed with sweetener.
Arrowroot	Arrow-root	Awowout	Used to thicken sauces. Ideal for sauces that do not need cooking.
Artichoke	Artichaut	Atisho	Green with leaves wrapping the heart. If leaves are spreading discolored, it is apt to be tough.
Avocado	Avocat	Zaboka	Green pear shaped fruit with a large seed in the middle. Very high in vitamin content and fat content.
Banana	Banane	Fig	Ripe when yellow. Good in salads or eaten alone.
Beets	Betterave	Bètrav	Boil to remove outer skin before using. Leaves make an excellent spinach substitute.
Breadfruit	L'arbre veritable	Lam veritab	6" to 8" diameter greenish brown or yellow when ripe. Meat must be cooked.

Common Food Names Translated (Cont.)

ENGLISH	FRENCH	CREOLE	DESCRIPTION AND USE
Breadfruit nut	L'Arbre a' pain	Labapen	Used as chestnuts. Roast or boil them and use in stuffings. Boil and sauté as a separate dish.
Broccoli	Brocoli	Bwokoli	Choose heads that are all green. If yellow appears, it is apt to be tough. Use in stir-fry, casserole, main dishes and steamed.
Cabbage	Chou	Shou	High source of vitamin C.
Cantaloupe	Mellon de France	Melon Frans	Large orangish fruit with grooves on sides. Ripe when grooves are yellowish and smells sweet.
Carrot	Carotte	Kawòt	Rich in vitamin A and potassium.
Cashew nut	Noix d'acajou	Nwa kajou	The yellow fruit of the cashew is a delicious treat that can be stewed with a light sweetener. Caution: the nut shells contain a strong irritant.
Cauliflower	Chou fleur	Shouflè	Rich in vitamins C, K and potassium. Good raw when well soaked.
Celery	Celeri	Seleri	Wild variety most readily available here is a wonderful seasoning.
Chayote	Mirliton	Militon	Green pear shaped squash. Good as a substitute for apples in desserts.
Chinese cabbage	Chou Chinois	Shou Shinwa	Long shaped cabbage. Delicious sautéed, in salads or in stir-fry dishes.
Chives	Cives	Siv	Member of the onion family. Used as a seasoning.

COMMON FOOD NAMES TRANSLATED (CONT.)

ENGLISH	FRENCH	CREOLE	DESCRIPTION AND USE
Coconut	Noix de coco	Kokoye	The meat is a source of protein & oil. The inner milky liquid from the fresh coconut is a good diuretic.
Coffee	Café	Kafe	Best from higher elevations. Haitian coffee is famous for its fine flavor.
Corn	Mais	Mayi	Dried corn variety. Ground into cornmeal.
Cucumber	Concombre	Konkonm	High water content. Contains vitamin A.
Custard apple	Cachiman	Kashiman	Heat shaped fruit with green or brown skins; the white pudding-like pulp of it makes very delicious eating.
Date	Datte	Dat	Rare in Haiti but delicious fresh or in pastries.
Dewberry	Framboise	Franbwaz	Tropical "raspberry". Used in jams and jellies. Serve fresh if cleaned well.
Eggplant	Aubergine	Berejèn	A purple skinned vegetable. High in water content.
Endive	Chicorée	Shikore	Similar to Chinese cabbage in looks. Long, prickly leaves. Use in salads or cooked with white sauce.
Fig	Figue	Fig Frans	Makes wonderful preserves.
Grapefruit	Pamplemousse	Panplemous	Round fruit with plenty of juice. Contains plenty of vitamin C and potassium.
Grapes	Raisins	Rezen	Small tropical varieties good for juice and jelly.
Grenadine	Grenadine	Grenadin	Large yellow fruit. Pulp can be put in blender with water and nutmeg for a delicious juice. A substitute for apples also.

COMMON FOOD NAMES TRANSLATED (CONT.)

ENGLISH	FRENCH	CREOLE	DESCRIPTION AND USE
Guava	Goyave	Gwayav	Round yellow fruit. Used in preserves, stewed or eaten fresh.
Heart of palm	Chou palmiste	Shou palmis	The inner heart of the palm tree. Used in salad sautéed, stir-fried, and in Chinese recipes.
Honeydew	Melon d'Espagne	Melon despay	Good source of vitamin B and C. Used in salads and desserts.
Leek	Poireau	Pwawo	A part of the onion family. White portion of vegetable is used. Makes for good seasonings.
Lettuce	Laitue	Leti	Lettuce, like all fresh leafy vegetables in Haiti, should be well soaked.
Lime	Citron	Sitwon	Rich in vitamin C. Substitute for lemons.
Mango	Mangue	Mango	Over 40 known varieties of mangoes in Haiti. The most renown is Madame Francique, which has a peach like pulp. Eat them fresh or in chutneys, preserves, and breads.
Manioc/Yuca	Manioc	Manyòk	Used to make cassava bread and tapioca.
Millet	Petit mil	Pitimi	A grain used as a substitution for rice or cornmeal.
Mulberry	Mur	Mi	Berries used fresh or in preserves.
Okra	Gombo	Kalalou	Used in sauces, soups, or deep-fried.
Onion	Oignon	Zonyon	The most important ingredient in Creole cooking.

COMMON FOOD NAMES TRANSLATED (CONT.)

ENGLISH	FRENCH	CREOLE	DESCRIPTION AND USE
Orange	Orange	Zoranj	The eating variety is yellow-green colored. The bright orange ones are sour and are used as a meat tenderizer.
Papaya	Papaye	Papay	Large orange and green fruit used fresh in salads and cooking. Leaves are used as a meat tenderizer.
Parsley	Persil	Pèsi	Two varieties, plain or curly leafed. Used in main dishes, sauces, seasoning and decorating.
Passion fruit	Grenadia	Grenadya	A small round, hard, green or purple skinned fruit. Has many seeds covered with a pulp used in fresh fruit drinks.
Peach	Pêche	Pèsh	Small wild and bitter variety. Used stewed or prepared in preserves.
Peanut	Arachide	Pistash	Rich source of protein and B vitamins. " Real" peanut butter must have hot pepper in it in Haiti
Peas	Petit pois	Pwa Frans	Usually much smaller than the imported variety, they require longer cooking time. Good source of vitamin A and phosphorous.
Pepper sweet bell	Poivron	Piman dous	Used in Creole dishes or stuffed with spicy ground meat and baked.
Habanero pepper	Piment	Piman bouk	Concentrated fire!
Pineapple	Ananas	Zanana	Buy one with a good aroma and when the top leaves pull out easily.

COMMON FOOD NAMES TRANSLATED (CONT.)

ENGLISH	FRENCH	CREOLE	DESCRIPTION AND USE
Plantain	Banane	Bannann	Variety of the banana family. Used in soups, fried, boiled, and main dishes. Usually green in color.
Plum	Prune	Prin	Wild variety - has a sour taste to it. Used in jellies and preserves.
Pomegranate	Grenade	Grenad	A thick-skinned, several-celled, reddish berry the size of an orange. Has many crimson colored seeds that have a tart flavor. The seeds are the part that you eat.
Potato	Pomme de terre	Pomdetè	Contain vitamins B, C and potassium. Haitian types boil better than North American varieties.
Pumpkin	Giroumont	Joumou	Round, speckled green skinned vegetable. Is mainly used here for soups but works well in dessert dishes, too.
Genip / Quenepe	Quenêpe, quenett	Kenèp	Clusters of small round green fruit. They are eaten by removing the outer shell and sucking off the pulp from the large pit.
Radish	Radis	Radi	The young green leaves are good cooked. Used in salads.
Rice	Riz	Diri	The favorite grain of Haiti.
Sapodilla	Sapountile	Sapoti	Small round brown skinned fruit about 2 ½" diameter. Has a delicious brown pulp with large black pits. Can be eaten fresh or used in preserves and sherbets.

COMMON FOOD NAMES TRANSLATED (CONT.)

ENGLISH	FRENCH	CREOLE	DESCRIPTION AND USE
Sesame seeds	Sesame	Wowoli	A wild variety can be obtained in the Iron Market. Must be cleaned well before using. Use in cooking and baking.
Shaddock	Chadèque	Shadèk	Round thick skinned citrus fruit with a point at one end. The juice is sour (substitute for grapefruit).
Shallot	Echalotte	Eshalòt	Used as seasoning, in sauces and in marinades.
Sorrel	Oseille	Lozèy	Adds a tangy taste to salads.
Soursop	Corossol	Kowosòl	A large green prickly-like fruit with a white pulp which is excellent in juice or in ice cream.
Spinach	Epinard	Zepina	Good source of vitamins A, C., iron & potassium.
Star Apple	Caimitte	Kayimit	Round shaped fruit found with either green or purple skins. The pulp is firm and white with a milky substance under the skin. Cut in half and eat with a spoon.
Strawberry	Fraise	Fryèz	You can find strawberries in both Kenscoff and in the Pine Forest.
String beans	Haricots verts	Pwatann	The variety most commonly available must have the strings removed before using.

COMMON FOOD NAMES TRANSLATED (CONT.)

ENGLISH	FRENCH	CREOLE	DESCRIPTION AND USE
Sugar cane	Canne à sucre	Kann	As a snack, with the skin removed and cut into pieces, the sweet juice is extracted by chewing the meat.
Sweet Potato	Patate	Patat	The true sweet potato. Bake, deep fry or puree.
Swiss chard	Carde Chinoise	Zepina gran fèy	Leafy green vegetable with white stem. Used in salad and prepared as you do spinach.
Tamarillo	Tamarillo	Tamariyo	An oval red fruit used in jams.
Tamarind	Tamarin	Tamaren	A sweet/sour fruit. Used in sauces, beverages, and butters. The tamarind leaves are used for curries.
Tangerine	Mandarine	Mandarin	A good source of vitamins A and C.
Taro	Malanga	Malanga	Large root. Used in soups or grated and used in fritter-type appetizers.
Tomato	Tomate	Tomat	Basic ingredient in Creole dishes and salads.
Turnip	Navet	Nave	Used raw with dips, pickled, grated in coleslaw or cooked in stews. Rich in vitamins A and C.
Watercress	Cresson	Kreson	Used fresh in salads, sandwiches or cooked in soups. Clean well before using.
Yam	Igname	Yanm	Yellow, white or tubers used pureed or in soups.
Zucchini	Courge	Eskwash/ koujèt	Can be eaten raw or cooked. Good for making pickles.

HERBS AND SPICES FOUND IN HAITI

ENGLISH	FRENCH	CREOLE	DESCRIPTION AND USE
Allspice	Malaguette	Malagèt	Aromatic spice used in baking, puddings, and drinks.
Basil	Basilic	Bazilik	Used in sauces.
Black pepper	Poivre	Pwav	Used in almost all food, except for desserts.
Camomille	Camomille	Kamomi	Makes a tea good for colic.
Celery	Celeri	Seleri	Rich in vitamins A, B, and C. Roots are diuretic.
Chives	Cive	Siv	Used in soups and dressings.
Cinnamon	Cannelle	Kanèl	Used in baking sweets and flavoring drinks.
Clove	Girofle	Jiwòf	Used in many Haitian dishes, to flavor sauces, meats, poultry, and desserts.
Garlic	Ail	Lay	Flavoring for meats, poultry, sauces, and soups.
Ginger	Gingembre	Jenjanm	Hot spicy flavor used in desserts, meat dishes and teas.
Hot pepper	Piment	Piman bouk	Spicy addition to meats and sauces.
Lemon balm	Melisse	Melis	For teas, soups, drinks - crushed leaves used for headaches.
Lemon grass	Citronelle	Sitwonèl	Makes a delightful tea - oil used against mosquitoes.
Mustard	Moutarde	Moutad	Used in pickles, salads, and dressings.
Nasturtium	Capucine	Kapisin	Leaf and flower edible, used in salads.
Nutmeg	Muscade	Miskad	Flavoring for sweets and drinks.
Onion	Oignon	Zonyon	Used in sauces, meats, poultry, and fish.
Parsley	Persil	Pèsi	Rich in iron - used in soups, salads and as a garnish.

HERBS AND SPICES (CONT.)

ENGLISH	FRENCH	CREOLE	DESCRIPTION AND USE
Peppermint	Menthe	Mant	Good for upset stomachs, flavoring, meats, and teas.
Rock Salt	Gros sel	Gwo sèl	Used in cooking. More nutritious than table salt.
Sage	Sauge	Souj	Flavoring in dressings and meats.
Salt	Sel	Sèl	Used in most foods. Gargle for sore throat.
Shallot	Echalote	Eshalòt	Onion-type spice used in meats and sauces.
Sorrel	Oseille	Lòzèy	Used in soups and salads.
Spearmint	Menthe	Tibom	Good for upset stomachs, flavoring, meats and teas.
Star anise	Anis etoile	Lani etwal	Used in candies, hot milk and tea.
Thyme	Thym	Ten	Used in most Haitian meat and rice dishes.
Vanilla bean/pod	Gousse de vanilli	Gous pwa vani	Flavoring for desserts, beverages, puddings.
Water cress	Cresson de fontaine	Kreson	Used in soups, salad and as garnishings.

MEATS AND SEAFOOD WITH TRANSLATION

	ENGLISH	FRENCH	CREOLE
BEEF	Brains	Cervelle	Sèvèl
	Cutlet	Escallope	Eskalòp
	Filet	Filet	Filè
	Ground round	Tartare	Vyan moulen sipeyè
	Hamburger	Viande hachée	Vyann moulen
	Liver	Foie	Fwa
	Roast	Rôti	Woti
	Rolled roast	Rôti de veau buttere	Woti / wotilad
	Sirloin steak	Faux filet	Fo Filè
	Soup bones	Jarret	Zo soup
	Stewing beef	Daube	Dob
	Tongue	Langue	Lang
PORK	Bacon	Butteron	Bekon
	Chops	Côtelette de porc	Kotlèt de pò
	Ham	Jambon	Janbon
	Loin (for griyo)	Carré de porc	Jigo pou fè griyo
	Ribs	Côtes	Kot de pò
	Sausage	Saucisse	Sosis

MEATS AND SEAFOOD (CONT.)

	ENGLISH	FRENCH	CREOLE
SEAFOOD	Barracuda	Barracuda	Begen, Taza
	Cod salted	Morue	Mori
	Conch	Lambi	Lanbi
	Crab	Crabe	Krab
	Crayfish	Crevette	Kribish
	Grouper	Merou	Pwason nèg
	Herring smoked	Hareng Saur	Aransò
	Lobster	Homard	Woma
	Oysters	Huître	Zwit
	Sardine	Sardine	Sadin
	Small fry	Pilchard	Piskèt
	Shrimp	Ecrevisse	Ekrevis
	Snapper	Sarde rose	Sad, Pwason woz
	Snook	Brochet	Bwochèt
MISC.	Chicken	Poulet	Poul
	Duck	Canard	Kana
	Frog legs	Cuisses de grenouilles	Kwis grenouy
	Goat	Chèvre	Kabrit
	Guinea fowl	Pintade	Pentad
	Lamb	Agneau	Mouton
	Pigeon	Pigeon	Pijon
	Rabbit	Lapin	Lapen
	Turkey	Dinde	Koden
	Turtle	Tortue	Tòti

INDEX

From Light Messages for those who love Haiti
Enjoy these books & share them with family and friends!

Hidden Meanings
Truth and Secret in Haiti's Creole Proverbs

Vant grangou fè lapriyè kout.
A hungry belly makes a short prayer.

- Featuring over 1200 proverbs, this is the best collection of the colorful proverbs that characterize Haiti and her people.

- Each of the photographs included with the text provides an additional window into the soul of Haiti and her people.

- Hardcover edition of over 250 pages containing more than 1200 entries.

Sòt pa touye 'w, men li fè ou swe.
Stupid doesn't kill you, but it makes you sweat.

Si tèt ou pa travay,
pye ou va travay.

If your head doesn't work; your feet will work.

Lord,

Help us not to talk too much.

Because talking too much is like driving too fast.

Sometimes the brakes are not good, and we pass by the place where we intended to stop.

God Is No Stranger (new expanded edition) is a prayer book unlike many others you may have seen. This book is unique because of the way these prayers reflect the childlike yet deep faith of a mountain people who have come to know God as a Friend acquainted with their culture and daily lives. These prayers are refreshing and heartwarming, sometimes almost humorous because of the homespun metaphors which are used. The photograph which accompanies each prayer tells a story by itself.

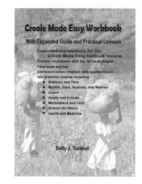

Creole Made Easy series – This short course is simply the easiest way to learn to speak Creole. The sixteen easy lessons in the *Creole Made Easy book* cover the basic elements of Creole grammar and pronunciation. A dictionary of over 4600 Creole to English and English to Creole translations is included.

The 2 CD set *Pronunciation Guide*, available separately, provides examples and practice in pronouncing Creole letters words, and sentences for each lesson in the book.

The optional *Creole Made Easy Workbook* accompanies the lessons of *Creole Made Easy* with additional tutorial and helps. The workbook also contains 7 additional chapters of survival Creole. These chapters include Numbers and Time, Months, Days, Seasons and Weather, Colors, Family and Friends, Marketplace and Food, Around the House, Health and Medicine.

Bèl Peyi Mwen
(My Beautiful Country)

Coloring book of Haitian scenes

Original drawings of scenes from everyday life in Haiti with text telling a story about rural life in Haiti.

Light Messages
www.lightmessages.com